THE DEAN'S LIST

THE DEAN'S LIST

Leading a Modern Business School

By Matthew A. Waller and Stephen Caldwell

epic.
books

FAYETTEVILLE

2021

CONTENTS

his book was written because it didn't exist. Obviously, this particular book didn't exist before I wrote it. But neither, as far as I could tell, did any other version that covered this topic well enough to really help me when I needed it most.

I was appointed interim dean of the Sam M. Walton College of Business at the University of Arkansas in 2015 and then dean in 2016. I quickly began the process of learning from the crucible of experience. I looked around for a book, guide, or some other resource that would equip me for the job. I found a few books about leading as a dean, but none of them provided much value. Three years later, I concluded that the book I wanted and needed didn't exist, so I decided to write it myself. Now you're reading it.

During those first few years, I saved almost every email I sent as dean, all the minutes from our executive committee meetings, and many other notes, articles, blogs, podcasts, and records that reflected some aspect of my leadership journey as dean. Reviewing them proved invaluable: I studied what was working and what wasn't. It helped me avoid repeating mistakes, improve on the things I did well, and figure out new and better approaches to a variety of challenges. All those notes became great resources as I wrote this book.

I hope the lessons I've learned about leading a college of business will equip you in your role as a leader—especially if you lead, or aspire to lead, a business school. It won't solve all your problems. I am still learning, so I don't have all of the answers. Plus, all deans face their own unique, unpredictable challenges, which means you'll still have to learn from your own crucible of experience. But I am confident this book will provide you with practical tools and insights that can help you lead more effectively and with greater confidence, regardless of your circumstances.

The book is segmented into three parts:

> **The Winding Road**—A little background about my journey will help you understand and make the most of the things you can learn from my approach to leading a business college.

The Solid Ground—These chapters cover my framework for leadership, not because my way is the only way to lead, but because it has served me well and because the principles are transferable to almost any leader in almost any setting. The framework is field-tested and proven, but flexible enough that you can adapt it to your personal preferences and style of leadership.

The 12-Lane Highway—This is where the proverbial rubber meets the road. I'll provide practical advice for dealing with the various specific challenges a dean regularly faces, all based on examples from my experiences and all in the context of my leadership framework. I'll also explore a few backroads along the way because leading a business college often takes you down uncharted paths, even if you have a great GPS.

My goal for this book is simple. I hope it shortens the learning curve for anyone who is or wants to be the dean of a business college. The way I see it, the less time deans spend figuring out how to lead and the more time they spend actually leading, the more successful they will be and the greater their influence. Deans have an incredible opportunity to have a positive influence on a wide range of audiences—students, parents, faculty, staff, administrators, alumni, business leaders, and the community. If this book adds value to that pursuit, then it was worth my time and effort. I already know at least one dean who benefited from it: me!

PART I

The Winding Road

My somewhat unconventional path to becoming a dean prepared me well for the demands of the job. Still, I had plenty to learn about what the role entails and how to do it effectively. The background on my journey in this section should give you some helpful context for my approach to leading a business college.

CHAPTER 1

An Inadvertent Dean

I don't know how many business school deans entered the workforce with a goal of becoming a business school dean, but I suspect the number is small. If there's a traditional path to this role, it probably begins mid-journey, when aspirations have been honed by time. Some might experience a moment or season when they say something along the lines of, "I'd like to be the dean of a business school." Then they chart their course much like any other leader looking to move into a specific role. I never experienced such a moment or season, so I never charted such a course. Yet, here I am, dean of the Sam M. Walton College of Business at the University of Arkansas.

Looking back, it's much easier to see how every twist and turn in my career path helped prepare me to lead the Walton College. In the moment, however, it often didn't make much sense to me at all.

I had no ambitions for an administrative position. I was always satisfied in the work I was doing as a teacher and researcher. The fact that I am among the top twenty most prolific researchers at the University of Arkansas (based on citations) tells you I can sit in an office all day long and be quite happy reading and writing. I love interacting with students and helping them learn and grow, but I've also always been a quiet person. Public speaking, a key skill for an academic administrator, was never my strength. Even the consulting I did tended to be rather quantitative in nature. So, it would have been no surprise if I had spent my entire career researching, writing, and teaching.

On the other hand, I've also been drawn to experiences outside of academia. My research led me to cofound two companies, one that provided consulting and the other that offered software related to my research as a supply-chain professor. This bent toward working with business leaders, as it turned out, was in line with a trend for business schools to use executive education as a revenue stream. As a result, doors of opportunity kept opening, and I kept walking through them, until one day I found myself walking through the door of the dean's office and realizing the chair inside it was mine.

It wasn't that simple, of course. But it's safe to say I never charted a course for the career I've actually experienced. And maybe it's just as well because I likely would have charted a very different course and ended up far less prepared.

The Deans' List

The Sam M. Walton College of Business has had 10 deans since 1926, as well as two interim/acting deans:

- Charles C. Fichtner (1926–1940)
- Karl M. Scott (1941–1943)
- Paul W. Milam (1944–1966)
- Acting Dean Merwyn G. Bridenstine (1966–1967)
- John P. Owen (1967–1983)
- Lloyd Seaton (1983–1989)
- Stan Smith (1989–1992)
- Interim Dean Thomas McKinnon (1992–1993)
- Doyle Z. Williams (1993–2005)
- Dan L. Worrell (2005–2012)
- Eli Jones (2012–2015)
- Matthew A. Waller (2015 to present)

I came to the University of Arkansas in 1994 as a visiting assistant professor and worked under three deans over the next twenty years. They were all very different, but all were very good leaders who moved the college in a positive direction. Not only did I learn from them about how to lead a business school, but they collectively laid the groundwork for much of the success that's taken place in the Walton College since I became dean.

Dan Worrell, the dean from 2005–2012, was the first to push me toward administration. One of his strengths was his willingness to take risks, and he took a risk with me.

At the time, I was a logistics professor in the department of marketing and logistics, and Dan recognized the growing importance of logistics and supply chain to our economy. The region surrounding the University of Arkansas is home to the world's largest company, Walmart, and one of the world's largest transportation and logistics companies, J.B. Hunt Transport

Services. It's also home to satellite offices for dozens of Walmart vendors, as well as the world headquarters of Tyson Foods. Anything related to supply chain management is especially relevant in our area of the country. Yet at that time we only graduated fifty students a year, and Dan bluntly asked me why our program was so small.

"Well, we're very constrained," I told him. "We don't have much faculty or freedom in how we manage the program."

Dan had been the chair of the management department at another university when it dealt with a very similar situation, so he recognized the need to give some independence to the discipline of supply chain management.

"There was a feeling in terms of the culture that they weren't as free as they should be to actually dive into their focus discipline because they had to play in this broader pond," Dan told me during a podcast we recorded in 2019. "When I looked at the marketing and logistics department, I saw a very similar thing. I saw that the logistics faculty were expected to contribute in marketing ways, even though that wasn't their home discipline. To me, that was a misalignment" (Waller 2019).

Given the common thread of supply chain that runs through companies like Walmart, Tyson, and J.B. Hunt, spinning off supply chain management as its own department became an obvious move, he said. Then he asked if I'd be willing to help create that department and lead it.[1]

The foundations were in place. John Ozment was a professor here who focused on logistics and supply chain management, and he recruited me to the University of Arkansas in 1994. The logistics program was very small, but John was a brilliant professor and cared deeply about his students and junior professors. He created impressive logistics projects for students in his classes and really equipped them to be effective in supply chain management. This, in turn, helped them become leaders in their companies after graduation and in the industry in general.

He also built great relationships with industry. In the late 1990s, John was the leader behind the creation of our Supply Chain Management Research Center (SCMRC). So between the alumni and the industry contacts through the SCMRC, we were well poised to create a new department.

---

1. In 2020, thanks largely to the efforts of Walton College Professor Remko Van Hoek, northwest Arkansas became home to the CSCMP Supply Chain Hall of Fame.

Still, moving forward with these ideas wasn't an easy choice. The country was experiencing the turbulent economic fallout of the Great Recession, and many were saying this was no time to start a new department. Universities are historically resistant to change, often moving, as Dan puts it, "at the speed of roadkill." Plus, I'd never aspired to run a department. I enjoyed teaching, research, executive education, and consulting. But he convinced me to take on the challenge.

Dan met face-to-face with every faculty member who would be asked to move into the new department, which included some from the Department of Information Systems who were more aligned with the topics of supply chain. He didn't force anyone to move, which meant everyone in the new department was aligned and bought into the change. And he met with the other department heads to address how the change would affect their budgets, among other concerns.

We also had to convince the provost, the chancellor, the president of the UA system, and the board of trustees that reorganizing the departments was a good idea. So one of the first things Dan asked me to do was to organize all the evidence I already had. Within a week, we received six or seven letters from top industry leaders at Walmart, FedEx Freight, and J.B. Hunt, among others, endorsing the idea of a separate supply chain department.

"In effect, these executives were carrying a lot of the water for our initiative," Dan told me. "These companies were also large donors to the university and had a very important footprint for the success of the university as a whole. So that was a very effective part of getting buy-in throughout the entire senior administration chain of command" (Waller 2019).

At Dan's request, I got similar letters from leaders within the UA, including support from the marketing department for spinning off logistics. With those letters in place, we put together a strategic plan explaining why there would be a demand among employers for these students and how we could address that demand.

Forward we moved, and eighteen months later, in July 2011, the UA had its Department of Supply Chain Management. We had to go through lots of hoops with the university, the board of trustees, and the state of Arkansas. But for the first time in decades, a new academic department had been birthed.

It was a small department, consisting of me, the other logistics faculty who had been in the marketing department, two professors who had been in the department of information systems, and a former executive with Procter & Gamble who helped with our strategic planning process and was served as our executive in residence. We grew quickly, however, and soon we were hitting on all cylinders when it came to research, teaching, outreach, and executive education.

I never thought I'd like being a department chair, but I soon considered it the best job I had ever held. The entrepreneur in me loved it. We benchmarked other programs across the country. We met with top leaders in supply chain management and logistics. We met with our faculty. We designed the curriculum. We crafted our mission, vision, strategies, tactics, and metrics.

We were inventing the future as we devised ways to add value in research and education. I realized that we had the opportunity to solve problems for companies who hired our students by giving our students an education that allowed them to think clearly, systematically, and innovatively. We had the opportunity to solve problems for companies with employees who were not sufficiently educated in key theoretical constructs that could help them describe, explain, and predict phenomena associated with supply chain management and logistics. We achieved these solutions through executive education. We had the opportunity to connect students with great companies by developing close relationships through our Supply Chain Management Research Center. The desire to solve problems for others is at the heart of an entrepreneur.

I also loved it because of my department faculty. They were smart, dedicated, and enjoyable to work with. This gave me the opportunity to learn from them and help them grow as researchers and teachers.

One of the reasons for our success overall was our success with executive education.[2] At one point, in fact, the top three hundred salespeople from J.B. Hunt enrolled in one of our executive education programs. This gave us extra money in our budget to reward faculty, market our department, and fund programs. We went from being the smallest major in the college

---

2. Associate Dean Brent Williams was an assistant professor at the time but he jumped in and worked to make our early executive education efforts successful. He was very involved in relationship development, event planning, and coordination and content delivery. I could see early on that he had a passion for executive education and was becoming an outstanding leader.

to the third largest (behind marketing and finance, based on the number of students graduated). As a result, we were sufficiently funded, and we had an unusual amount of visibility in the industry. Consequently, we began attracting top professors, including some who gave up tenured positions elsewhere to join our team.

In 2012, Dan resigned as dean so he could spend more time with his wife and mother because both of them were going through serious illnesses. After a national search, the UA hired Eli Jones as the new dean of the business college, and Eli and I quickly hit it off. A year later, Eli nominated me for the prestigious SEC leadership development program. I became one of four faculty members from the UA who were chosen because we were considered to have a high potential for senior administrative leadership. I had no plans of going above my role as department chair, but I valued the experience. I figured learning more about things like budgeting processes and how other universities operated would help me lead the Supply Chain Department.

Eli also loved what we were doing with executive education for supply chain, and he wanted to replicate it throughout the rest of the college. He offered to create a new associate dean position for me so that I could lead that effort. Again, I was reluctant to make the move. For one thing, I loved what I was doing. For another, the only other full professor in our department was about to retire. There was no one in the internal pipeline to replace me as the department chair.

You can do both, Eli told me. *I'll get you funds for an extra assistant department chair to help do what you need to do. You can run the strategic parts of the department and be associate dean for executive education.*

I don't know if I'd like that, I told him.

OK, I'll make you interim, he said, *so if you don't like it, you can go back.*

He made it almost impossible to say no, so I stepped through that door and embraced the new challenges and opportunities that came with it. I would imagine that in most departments in business schools the faculty in a department would object to a part-time department chair, but not in our department. I talked about it with each member, and each was supportive.

Not long after I became associate dean, Texas A&M University had an opening for the dean of its prestigious Mays Business School. Eli had grown up in College Station, Texas, and had earned three degrees from Texas A&M, so it was his dream job. Naturally, he applied for it, and he landed the position in April 2015. This is when my world really began to change at break-neck speed. First, Eli began recruiting me to join him at Texas A&M to run the Aggies' executive education program. Second, the UA asked me to step in as interim dean of the Walton College.

My immediate reaction to both options was to stick with the status quo. I didn't think I was ready to serve as dean, even on an interim basis. I had some idea of the demands of the job. I knew it would require me to stretch my leadership skills well beyond my comfort zone, especially when it came to communications. And I knew it would suck time away from my wife and our four children—two in college, one in high school, and one in junior high.

The prospect of going to Texas A&M with Eli turned out to be more attractive than I expected. I have a great deal of respect for Eli and loved working for and with him. Plus, Texas A&M has a terrific business college with a well-established executive education program.

What made the decision even more difficult was that I had a great experience in College Station when my wife, Susanne, and our youngest daughter, Sarah, went down for a visit. The faculty of the operations department threw a party for me, and we had a ton of fun. They not only were unbelievable scholars, but great people to spend time with. Many of them lived in the same neighborhood, and they all got along really well. The next day, I made a presentation, and everyone made me feel welcome and wanted.

I figured I would get resistance from my family, especially from our youngest son. At the time, Luke was doing very well in high school, had close friends, and was the starting strong safety for the Fayetteville High School football team—a team that would end up winning the state championship his junior and senior years. But he was willing to make the move, as was my wife and our daughter who was still at home.

When all was said and done, however, we realized it simply wasn't time to leave Fayetteville.

Shortly after making that decision, I got a call from Sharon Gaber, at the time the provost at the University of Arkansas, asking me to become interim dean of the Walton College. I told her I wasn't interested in the job, but she called back a week later and asked me again.

What do we have to do to make it happen? she said.

The more I thought about it, the more it seemed like a good option.

I always think I'm not going to like the next job, I said to myself, *but I always do.*

So in June 2015 I assumed the role of interim dean of the Walton College of Business.

I wasn't sure if I would apply for the permanent job, nor was there any guarantee that I would get it if I did. One of the unpredictable factors was that other changes also were taking place in the UA administration. Chancellor David Gearhart retired in July 2015, meaning we would have an interim chancellor until someone new was hired. And Sharon Gaber, the provost who had offered me the interim dean position, left that same month to become president of the University of Toledo.

I didn't know who would pick the next dean, so I had no idea how long I would hold the office, but I committed from the start to run the college as if there were nothing interim about it. Within two months, I was getting offers to apply as dean for openings at other business colleges. More importantly, I realized I liked this job better than any I'd ever held. I find joy in seeing students succeed, and I'm convinced that business makes the world a better place. So I decided I would formally apply for the position, and then I waited to see who the UA would hire as its next chancellor.

When that announcement came on October 23, 2015, I made what some considered a bold move—I went to meet the new chancellor before he could come to meet with me. Joseph Steinmetz would not assume his new duties until January 1, 2016, so he was still provost and vice-chancellor of academic affairs at The Ohio State University on the Friday when the press release went out saying he was coming to Arkansas. I immediately called his assistant and asked if I could meet with him that next week if I was willing to fly to Columbus, Ohio. She politely told me he didn't have any openings in his schedule. I pressed a little harder and she said she would see what she could do. She called back a few minutes later and told me Steinmetz could meet with me that Monday from 5:30 to 6 p.m.

As you might expect, Steinmetz was a bit guarded when our meeting began. But in short order we were laughing and talking like old friends. We talked about the history of the University of Arkansas, how various functions worked within the university, key constituents, and, of course, the history and future of the Walton College. He was asking me all sorts of questions about Fayetteville and the university, and our thirty-minute meeting ended up lasting nearly two hours. To this day, we have a great relationship.

Steinmetz had helped Ohio State search for a business school dean in 2014, so he was well-prepared to lead the search for the next dean of the Walton College. He began that search when he arrived on campus in January by looking over my vita with Ashok Saxena, who had assumed the role of provost. Then he called a meeting with the faculty of the business school and told them he could do a national search but that he felt confident that I was the best candidate. In fact, he said many other top candidates wouldn't bother applying once they knew I was being considered. I certainly felt honored that he would say it, and it bolstered my confidence.

The faculty agreed to keep the search internal, but no other internal candidates applied. I still had to go through the process and make several formal presentations. But with strong support within the college, across the university, and from external leaders in the business community, the interim tag was removed.

I had tremendous support from the chancellor, the provost and everyone around me. I had a great team around me, a great faculty, and a great foundation that was laid by the previous deans. If I didn't succeed, there would only be one person to blame—me. So I got to work, determined to make the best of the best job I have ever had.

CHAPTER 2

Chief of Ten

R ichard Armour, an English professor known mostly for his poetry, magazine articles, and satirical books, spent the early 1960s as dean of faculty at Scripps College in Claremont, California. Given his love for words, one of the first things he did when he took that job was to study the origins of his new title.

He quickly learned that *dean* came from the Latin *decanus,* meaning "chief of ten." It originally described a Roman soldier leading a unit of ten members who all shared the same tent. Later, it was used by the church to designate someone who oversaw ten monks in a monastery. The church, of course, gave us modern academia, and the title of *dean* came along for the ride.

This was interesting stuff to Armour, so he eagerly shared his etymological knowledge with another dean of faculty during a speaking engagement at a larger university. The other dean, upon learning the background of the word, "slapped his forehead," according to Armour, and then "blurted out, 'Oh, to have only ten to look out for, and to have even one of them a monk!'" (Armour 1980).

The duties of a dean, it seems, have changed dramatically over time, and who's to say it's more difficult to oversee a college faculty than a group of monks or soldiers? But as the tenth dean of the Sam M. Walton College of Business at the University of Arkansas—sort of the "tenth chief" rather than the "chief of ten"—I can tell you academic deans face some unique challenges in our increasingly complex and dynamic roles.

Some of those challenges, of course, aren't particularly new. The deans of business schools—or any schools, for that matter—have always had to navigate the often-choppy internal administrative waters of a university. They've had to manage up, down, and sideways while dealing with students, staff, senior administrators, and tenured and nontenured faculty.

Allan Tucker and Robert Bryan, in their 1991 book *The Academic Dean,* characterized the role of the dean as "dove, dragon, and diplomat." (I take that to mean deans are at least partly mythical creatures.)

Over the last ten or so years, however, the role of a dean, especially in high-profile business colleges, has taken an increasingly external focus. While deans still face all the challenges that come with leading in a shared governance model, the job is more and more like that of a CEO of a large company and the leader of a start-up company combined. In addition to the internal stakeholders, there's a growing demand to work with parents, alumni, donors, business leaders, and community leaders.

In 2016, *The Chronicle of Higher Education* produced a focus report, "How to Be a Dean." Audrey Williams June pointed out in the opening article that most colleges seeking a dean twenty years ago simply pulled the best administrator from the internal ranks. Deans today, however, must be "part entrepreneur, part fundraiser, part marketer, and part seasoned administrator . . . with the ability to build partnerships and develop strong new programs capable of generating revenue" (June 2018).

Modern deans, according to June, "have their hands on more levers than almost anyone else on campus," which makes them influential agents of change. "As leaders of increasingly complex enterprises, deans must think big and be the public face of their schools even as they still tend to the day-to-day needs of professors and students," June wrote. "Deans must be able to motivate faculty and staff to embrace a university's broad, strategic goals. They need to be shrewd money managers who can attract donations to augment limited budgets" (June 2018).

I was hesitant to take the job as interim dean because I was aware of many of the challenges that came with the role. And the longer I sat in that chair, the longer that list grew. I'll never forget one phone call in particular I had with the dean of another business college who mentioned that many deans don't realize the amount of personal liability that comes with the job. Deans, he told me, often get sued by faculty over disagreements about promotions and tenure. They can also be held liable for incidents like sexual misconduct within a department. And deans are financially liable because they manage purchases and operate a huge budget for a quasi state entity, which means there are a host of laws that apply to their college that don't apply to other businesses.

Other deans told me I could expect to lose all discretion over my time because of the nonstop meetings. And by the way, I'd now be responsible for raising huge amounts of money, which, of course, required lots of meetings and came with tons of pressure to hit goals.

The more I learned about the expectations, roles, responsibilities, and liabilities that came with the job, the more overwhelming it all felt.

Edward Snyder, who served as dean of the business or management schools at the University of Virginia, the University of Chicago, and Yale University, told *The Wall Street Journal* that the role of dean is growing increasingly more difficult because, "The expectations of the various constituencies you serve have all dialed up, and it keeps getting a little more difficult to meet those expectations" (Gee 2018).

At the time of the article's publication—June 2018—Snyder had just announced plans to return to a faculty position beginning in 2019, making Yale one of at least ten major US universities that were searching for a new dean of their business school. Others included Cornell University, Notre Dame University, the University of California at Los Angeles, and the University of California at Berkeley.

As those positions were filled, others opened. At the end of 2018, there were forty-five postings on higheredjobs.com for business school deans, and in January 2020 the number was roughly the same—forty-eight openings.

There are a lot of openings partly because there are a lot of business colleges. In fact, there are more than 16,500 business schools around the world, according to the Association to Advance Collegiate Schools of Business (AACSB), including 1,619 in the United States. The average tenure of a dean of those colleges is just 5.9 years (Sholderer 2018).

Here's how we can connect those dots: There are thousands of business schools, and leading those schools is increasingly challenging. Many deans feel ill-equipped to handle the complex and dynamic environments and relationships that come with the job. The expectations are high, the hours are long, and the pressure is intense. They give it their best but leave after a few years. Some move up but others often move back into teaching and research positions.

The way I saw it when I got the job—and the way I still see it—my role as the leader of the Walton College is pretty simple: My number one job is to fulfill the college's vision and mission, and do it in a way that upholds our stated values. Those formalized statements—the vision, mission, and values—are my mandate. My motives, thoughts, words, actions—everything I do as dean—should align with this mandate. If I don't do that, I'm failing.

Of course, there's more to succeeding as a dean than understanding the role. It's a great place to start, but just because I can view the role in simple terms doesn't make the job easy. I still have to execute in that role, and that's where it can get complicated. To fulfill the Walton College mandate, I have to effectively lead and manage the people inside, outside, and all around the college in ways that deliver positive results. And therein lies the challenge.

I am still learning as I go, but I have learned enough to reach this conclusion: To successfully lead and manage a college of business, you must commit the elements of your mandate (vision, mission, values) into your leadership DNA and be able to apply that mandate within the context of a viable, well-understood leadership-management framework. That's the premise of this entire book.

I'm going to share the framework I have developed. It gives me guidance for what I need to do (and not do) as a leader, the skills and capabilities I need to develop as a leader, and how to lead in a constantly changing environment.

I'll explain what I mean by committing the mandate into my leadership DNA and why that's important to any framework. As I describe and unpack the framework, I'll share practical examples of how it has served me as a dean. And in the final section of the book, I'll go deeper into some of the leadership challenges and opportunities deans routinely face in specific areas. These include creating, socializing, and marketing a strong brand narrative; developing the right structure, strategy, and priorities; promoting diversity; funding the vision, both through donor and non-donor sources; and communicating messages that inform, equip, and encourage the people a dean needs to influence.

I have worked for some remarkable deans during my career—Doyle Williams, Dan Worrell, and Eli Jones—and those experiences proved valuable when I became dean. In addition, I've been a student of leadership for years, both as an academic and as a practitioner running my own companies and academic units.

The leadership model I apply is a result of my studies, my observations, and my experiences, all of which include successes and failures along the way. I recognize that different people have different personalities and different perspectives, and that there is no singular, perfect model for leading. But I'm convinced that this approach and the lessons I've learned will help any dean of a college, and especially any dean of a business school, achieve success in the modern academic environment. And while much of the content is focused on leading in a business school, the approach also works well in just about any other leadership environment—even if you lead soldiers or monks.

PART II

The Solid Ground

Every leader is unique. Certain principles of leadership, however, apply to anyone who wants to have a positive influence on others and help them achieve their personal and collective common goals. The leadership framework I use fits my style. How you bring these principles to life might differ based on your personal style, but they are transferable. Understanding how I've applied this framework will lead you to a deeper understanding of the lessons I've learned about leading. That, in turn, will allow you to adapt the elements of my framework to fit your needs and apply it to specific challenges that you're also likely to face as a business college dean.

CHAPTER 3

A Leader's DNA

I mentioned earlier that my number one job as dean is to fulfill the vision and mission of the Sam M. Walton College of Business, and do it in a way that upholds our stated values. The mission and vision answer our "Why?" question—Why do we exist as a college?—and the values help ensure our ends won't justify our means. The mandate is the filter that guides decisions and helps set priorities on everything from hiring practices to strategic direction and major initiatives. So if the framework that I'll outline later is the bones of my approach to leadership, the mandate is the very heart and soul.

The mission, vision, and values must stay on the tip of my tongue as I go about my day. All the decisions I'm making and all of my interactions should be filtered through the lens of that mandate because those conversations and decisions influence where the college ends up. But that influence will never happen if I don't know it—and I mean *really, really* know it. The mandate isn't just written on a card in my wallet, it's written on my heart. It's not just engraved on a plaque that hangs on my wall, it's ingrained in my mind. I never have to look it up when I need to type it or say it word-for-word.

Given its importance, memorizing the mandate is Task No. 1 when a dean takes office. The ability to simply recall the components of the mandate verbatim like a programmed robot, however, won't produce the level of understanding I'm talking about here. The elements of an organization's mandate have to be deeply embedded in a leader's mind and heart. That said, memorizing the mandate verbatim is essential to grafting it into your leadership DNA and successfully achieving that deep-level commitment.

So, for the record, here it is . . . from memory (I promise):

The mission of the Sam M. Walton College of Business is to advance and disseminate business knowledge using a diverse, inclusive, and global perspective and to encourage innovation in our primary strategic endeavors: Retail, Data Analytics, and Entrepreneurship.

The vision: *Through our teaching, research, and service, the Sam M. Walton College of Business will be a thought leader and a catalyst for transforming lives in Arkansas, the United States, and the world.*

The values are EPIC:

- *Excellence: We are driven to be the best in everything we do.*
- *Professionalism: We operate with integrity, humility, respect, and inclusion.*
- *Innovation: We imagine possibilities, we create, and we inspire others.*
- *Collegiality: We respect each individual, we value our differences, and we welcome all.*

You will see strands of this mandate woven throughout this entire book because the mandate is part of my leadership DNA, and that doesn't happen by accident.

Memorizing the mandate is the first step toward understanding all of the components held within it, toward living them out myself, toward communicating them formally and informally, and toward bringing them to life. The mission and vision provide the destination, and the values set the boundaries. Then we can aggressively and responsibly create the strategy for getting where we want to go.

Our faculty, in keeping with our shared governance model, developed the vision, mission, and values before I became dean, but we didn't have a fully developed strategic plan when I took office. The vision, for instance, instructs us to be a "thought leader" and a "catalyst for transforming lives." That left me with an obvious question as a new leader: *How do we do that?* A clearly articulated strategy would help us answer that question.

In the companies I had founded, that type of strategic plan evolved somewhat organically over time. The Walton College, however, needed to proactively develop a formalized approach that matched the established mandate. So, I asked one of our faculty members, Vikas Anand, to work with the faculty on strategic initiatives that supported our vision and mission. They came up with seven initiatives—research, teaching, diversity and inclusion, globalization, analytics, entrepreneurship, and retail and supply chain—and I memorized those, as well. Next, we began creating a strategic plan and priorities around those initiatives.

Commitment Matters

Some leaders believe it's unnecessary to actually memorize their mission, vision, or values. *I need to know what they are,* they say, *but there's no need to commit them to memory. The important thing is to apply them. That's what really matters.*

Application, of course, is the critical end goal. But leaders who take that approach inevitably fail to consistently apply their mandates in the very moments when it matters most.

Andy Stanley, in *Next Generation Leader,* points out, "There is no cramming for a test of character. It always comes as a pop quiz. You're either ready or you're not." The same is true when it comes to your mandate. You don't know when you will be tested on it, but you can rest assured that the pop quizzes will come, so you can't afford to procrastinate.

When you're leading in meetings, you don't have time to go look up the mandate to see how it applies to the pointed question someone just shot in your direction like an arrow from the bow of Apollo . . . or Legolas, if you prefer *The Lord of the Rings* to Greek mythology. If you aren't prepared, you might do your best to fend off the arrows. Later, as you're sitting alone at your desk and you no longer feel under attack, you might reflect on the mandate and the answers to those pointed questions will become clear. Or perhaps you never get around to reflecting on the mandate because you're too consumed with frustration over how the meeting progressed.

When the mandate is fully committed—when it's part of who you are as a leader—you can contemplate it as you're going along on your morning run, as you're driving during your commute, or as you're reading through the headlines. You can think through what it means and how it applies to a broad range of situations. Then you can apply it during discussions in ways you never might have imagined, which can come in handy if a meeting resembles the Trojan War.

Frankly, it wasn't easy for me to memorize our mandate, much less commit it into my leadership DNA. Let's face it, it's not the simplest 120 words that have ever joined forces into six sentences. But it's a precise, carefully crafted group of words, and every one of them matters—to the college, but also to me personally. I truly *believe* in our mandate.

So, I recited those words aloud, over and over. I wrote them out by hand, again and again. And again. Day after day after day. Week after week after week. Before long, I had the elements of the mandate memorized with stone-cold precision. And once I got them down, I made sure I didn't forget them. Memorizing a passage is like developing our muscles. We can build them up, but they atrophy if they aren't regularly exercised. Committing the mandate isn't something you achieve, but something you're always in the process of achieving.

10 Tips for Committing Your Mandate
1. Memorize the mandate verbatim.
2. Consider current initiatives and resource allocations of the organization, and practice explaining why they facilitate or deter from the mandate.
3. When writing emails to people in the organization about decisions, include relevant aspects of the mandate and use logic to connect the decisions to the mandates.
4. When making presentations to the organization, recite parts of the mandate and explain how what you are presenting relates to the mandate or parts of the mandate.
5. Ask people to discuss the mandate with you.
6. Find out which elements of the mandate are measured and how they are measured. If any elements aren't measured, find out why.
7. Ask your leadership team to describe how parts of the mandate are being achieved and how parts are being neglected.
8. Open meetings by reciting parts of the mandate and explain why the meeting pertains to the mandate.
9. When a decision is made to support a new initiative or to provide resources to a new initiative, tie it to the mandate both verbally and in writing.
10. When a decision is made to not support a new initiative, explain the decision in light of the mandate. If a contrary argument is made that the initiative would actually support the mandate, then listen carefully. You might want to take some time, think about it, and then reply later.

I make it a practice to apply the different aspects of our mandate regularly in written and oral communications, to think through them during my decision making, and to cite them (often verbatim) during discussions throughout the week with students, faculty, staff, administrators, alumni, business leaders, and anyone else who enters my sphere of influence. When I write emails to the college, many times I explain my subject in the context of the mandate—how it is based on our values or supports our strategic initiatives. I start many of our meetings by

restating the mandate. I frequently think about how it applies to decisions I am making. And I often explain how it applies to resource-allo-
cation decisions.

Very few of our students, faculty, or staff fully commit the mandate to
memory. But they encounter it often enough to know how important it
is and to recognize it whenever it comes up. The "Be Epic" tagline is the
screensaver on the computers in our labs, and we often use the #BeEpic
hashtag in our social media posts that exemplify our mandate in some way.
You can search that hashtag on Twitter, LinkedIn, Instagram, and Facebook
to find our posts. Our mission, vision, and values appear below my signature on the college emails. They are a significant marketing message for the
college—you'll see them on elevator doors, on signs in our hallways, on
our webpages, in our social media posts, in our magazine, and just about
anywhere else we can think to post them. And if you're around me, our
mandate will come up early and often because I have it memorized and
committed, and because I eagerly share it.

It can feel really awkward when you first start doing this, because it can
feel like it's fake. But after you practice a while, it becomes a comfort. Using
that mandate for all that it's worth becomes natural and instinctive. Most
of all, it's effective.

Why? Well, there are at least three reasons why every dean should commit the mandate into his or her leadership DNA.

One, it takes the drama out of decision making.

Peter Northouse, a professor emeritus in the School of Communication
at Western Michigan University, wrote, "Leadership is a process whereby
an individual influences a group of individuals to achieve a common goal"
(Northouse 2018).

That's probably my favorite definition of leadership because it emphasizes the process over the characteristics of the leader. When we commit
the mandate, we improve the process for influencing individuals to achieve
the common goal. And when the committed mandate is applied over and
over in an informed manner, the organization can move forward quickly,
thoroughly, and with few distractions.

By the time I had held my role as dean for a year or two, you could throw
anything at me, and I could use the vision, mission, and values to either
support or reject doing it. That's still the case today. I can make an informed

decision that's in the best interest of the college because I am confident that decision aligns with and supports the mandate.

Imagine someone stops me in the hallway and says, "It occurs to me that everyone in the Walton College needs new business cards that are really small, because smaller cards are more sustainable." Personally, I might find that a great idea. As the dean of the Walton College, however, it doesn't fit our mandate.

"The vision of the college is to be a thought leader and a catalyst for transforming lives," I could say. "I don't see how smaller business cards accomplished that. Therefore, it's not going to be one of my focus areas unless you can show me how it aligns with our mandate."

On the other hand, the mandate often draws me to advocate for ideas.

In 2018, for instance, I was evaluating our role as thought leaders. *What does it really mean to be thought leaders,* I wondered, *and how well are we achieving that objective?* Our faculty publishes academic articles all the time, of course, but many of those test existing theories. They aren't futuristic. We attend conferences, we often present on trends, and we frequently consult with business leaders. But I felt like we needed to do more.

So one of the things we did to expand our role as future-focused thought leaders was launch a series of forums on industry trends. The first one focused on domestic freight transportation. The participants included top executives from Fortune 500 retail, food, freight, and logistics companies, as well as business professors, a venture capitalist specializing supply chain, and a world-renowned producer of economics media.

We spent a couple of hours coming up with insights into what leaders should do about the most significant existing and emerging trends that would likely still be part of the business in ten years. A year later, we held a similar event that focused on the future of the forestry industry, and the year after that we were planning one on banking.

These forums result in blogs and articles we can publish or use with students in the classroom. They also result in ideas the executives can apply in their businesses. And they strengthen the Walton College's brand as a for-ward-thinking partner that helps shape, not just study, business. Putting on these forums has a cost, but the decision to launch them was easy, because they fit perfectly with our mandate.

As another example, leaders of our Department of Information Systems approached me a few years ago with an idea for forming a center with a focus on blockchain technology. At the time, however, the university had just opened several new academic centers. The central administration had said it didn't want us to form any new academic centers in the immediate future and that some existing centers should actually be closed.

Saying no to a center that focused on blockchain would have been an easy choice given that directive. But when I filtered the idea through our mandate, the decision to advocate for it made perfect sense. It fit perfectly with our mission and vision, and I was able to articulate it in those terms when I presented the idea to our central administration. Those leaders listened, asked insightful questions, and then agreed that it was worth an exception. We opened the Blockchain Center for Excellence in 2018, and it's helping us stay on the cutting edge of research and application of blockchain technology, specifically as it applies to business.

Two, it creates shared buy-in.

There's been a ton of research in recent years about the benefits of creating a culture in which people find meaning in their work that goes beyond dollar amounts on paychecks. Yet, research also indicates that even well-meaning executives often don't do a good job of clearly articulating their organization's purpose and values and, therefore, their workers aren't as engaged and productive as they could be.

Dan Cable and Freek Vermeulen, who have researched and written extensively on this topic, came up with four "organizational-design interventions" to help build a culture that personalizes change, and committing the organization's mandate supports two of their interventions—helping people grasp the impact of their work and connecting work to a higher meaning (Cable and Vermeulen 2018).

By making the mandate part of my leadership DNA, I routinely share, with words and actions, the impact of our work and the connection to a higher meaning. This keeps everyone aligned to our shared vision and inspires them to move toward it. When a leader helps the organization move toward what it wants to become, others will want to be part of that journey.

As I noted earlier, the faculty came up with the elements of our mandate, not I. I'm just applying them. The faculty also decided our strategic direction. I'm just making sure we stay on that highway. My commitment to knowing that mandate by memory and applying it to my leadership as dean strengthens the buy-in, because it provides daily proof that I respect the wishes of the faculty and that I'm working on their behalf. The faculty sees my buy-in, which helps confirm that the mandate is worthwhile and motivates them and others to live it themselves.

They not only buy in more fully to the mandate but also to the decisions that are made when the mandate is used as a filter. Knowing that decisions throughout the college are vetted by the mandate helps limit resistance to those decisions. They realize that decisions, especially those coming from the dean's office, aren't unduly influenced by typical collegiate politics. Confidence and trust develops, which results in less complaining about choices that may go against the personal preferences of people who will need to live by those decisions.

I made it clear to the Information Systems Department that I was supporting the Blockchain Center for Excellence because it advanced our mission. I wanted them to know, because I want that reality to permeate our culture. I suspect everyone who works around me knows that I have our mission, vision, and values memorized, and that causes them to think those elements through more often. They realize if they're going to win with me, they've got to do a very good job of contextualizing whatever they're talking about within the strategic direction of the college. That means they typically come to me with pre-filtered ideas—they share their idea and how it supports the mandate. That's how they get buy-in from me, and that's how I gain buy-in from others.

Three, it positions you to defend or change your mandate.

Memorizing the mandate not only makes it easier to make decisions and create buy-in but also positions you to change the elements of the mandate when necessary. In fact, if I took a position of leadership in any organization, the first thing I would do is memorize the mission, vision, and values—even if I wanted to change them. It's much easier to make the case for change if you have mastered an understanding of what it is you want changed. If you don't know the mandate extremely well, people can out debate you on the need for change. Knowledge truly is power.

I am the only person I know of in the Walton College who has all these elements memorized. Several people know them in principle or have a great feel for their content, but they can't recite them word for word on the spot. I've also memorized our strategic initiatives and our metrics. Anybody who's talking to me is at a huge disadvantage in a disagreement because I can tie everything back to a mandate that was crafted by our faculty. Who's going to say, "We don't want to fulfill our mission"? Memorizing the mandate might not make me Apollo, but it gives me the arrows I need to defend or change the mandate.

At the same time, leaders who have committed the mandate still need to seek the opinions of others. In fact, continually seeking diverse opinions on issues affected by the mandate increases the degree to which the mandate is committed, makes leaders more informed, and helps them lead more effectively. Having the mandate deeply committed can be dangerous if you become rigid in your application, so it is important to continually discuss it with others. You want to be sturdy but not unyielding in the application of the mandate.

Changing any parts of the mandate without a deep understanding of them is an injustice to the organization that created them. Leaders owe it to the organization and its stakeholders to carefully and thoroughly contemplate any aspect of the mandate we think should be changed. After that, if it is still clear that a change is needed and we have explored it with the leadership of the organization and other stakeholders, then we need to be decisive in making the change while also carefully constructing a just process for making it.

The Gauges of Leadership

A fascinating aspect of our vision and values is how they are tied together through our tagline—Be epic.

The word *epic* traditionally means a long poem about the heroic deeds and adventures of some legendary leader or group. Our epic is our story, our shared adventure, and its heroes are our faculty, staff, students, and alumni.

Today, in the colloquial sense, epic also means *great*. The double meaning is even more reflective of our mandate, and the tagline connects the vision and values.

Be an epic thought leader. Be an epic catalyst for transforming lives. Exemplify excellence, professionalism, innovation, and collegiality in all that you do—as a student, as a faculty or staff member, as an administrator, and as an alumnus.

When I see evidence of those values taking root and producing fruit in our culture, I know we're well positioned to achieve our short- and long-term goals. I see this evidence in the decisions and behaviors of our people, of course, but sometimes the signs are less obvious.

In 2019, for instance, we were in the process of forming the Department of Strategy, Entrepreneurship and Venture Innovation (SEVI) out of our Department of Management. The changes were so significant that it resembled creating two new departments. We were creating new leadership structures, and some faculty and staff were transitioning to different roles with new responsibilities.

Former Dean Dan Worrell was interim chair of the Department of Management, but John Delery (management) and Jon Johnson (SEVI) were the faculty members leading the transition. It was an epic challenge that required them to stay true to our EPIC values. Gary Peters, chair of the Department of Accounting, took the time to email a document to Delery and Johnson that he thought would support their efforts.

"This was a statement of EPIC Dept Chair Commitments that the E-Committee put together a few years ago," Gary told them in an email he shared with me. "I have found it very helpful when attempting to straddle one foot in administration and one foot in faculty. I actually keep a copy posted outside my door."

The document described how a Walton College department chair lives out each value, with four to six bullet points for each value. (There's a similar document for the dean and assistant deans; see Appendixes A and B.) To me, the email was a reminder that our values, like the rest of the mandate, have to be part of our DNA. Gary wasn't telling his colleagues they should post the values outside their door. He was telling them that keeping the EPIC values top of mind is invaluable when making decisions as a department chair. That's how values become ingrained in our culture.

My commitment to knowing our mandate (including the values) not only guides my decision making but also helps me easily see whether the mandate is guiding the decisions and behaviors of faculty, staff, and students throughout the college. I see whether it's taking root and producing fruit. And I'm constantly monitoring the evidence.

Often, leadership resembles piloting an airplane. You constantly need to monitor the gauges in front of you and respond to the information they provide. The mandate, however, isn't just a gauge to monitor. It's an organization's essence, something that you need to deeply know and understand to effectively move the organization where it needs to go.

Like the experienced pilot, it's the nuanced and subtle elements you consider about the aircraft and flying conditions that allow you to make more informed, intelligent decisions that will get you and your organization through the turbulence and land you at your destination.

CHAPTER 4

Framing a Leadership Approach

A leader in any new role begins by making some basic assessments, and that's what I did when I became dean of the Walton College. There's a tendency to start by assessing the organization—the strengths and weaknesses of people and structures, the obvious problems that need fixing, the strategy and policy changes that need making. Those are important areas to evaluate, regardless of whether you are new to the organization or have seen it from the inside for years.

For me, however, it began with two very inward-focused, interrelated questions: What's my role? What's my philosophy and framework for leading? Unless I understood the answers to those questions, I wouldn't be ready to respond very well to any of the other assessments I could make of myself or others.

Knowing the mandate helps leaders gain a clear understanding of where an organization wants to go and why. It also helps them make decisions about how to get there. But we also need a consistent framework for operating as a leader. I believe that framework rests on the foundation of who the leader is—what we believe as leaders and how we see the world and our place in it. The philosophy sets the nonnegotiable parameters for building a framework, and together they provide a structure for successfully executing a plan to fulfill the mandate.

My philosophy of leadership is born out of my personal faith. It's a servant leadership approach that places an enormous value on the inherent worth of other people. I believe people matter—even people I don't agree with or who do things I don't like. At the core of my faith is a deep sense of gratitude for the fact that God loves me despite my many imperfections. That gratitude compels me to love others, to forgive others, to sacrifice for others, and to serve others. I don't always do all of those things, of course, but I believe that the more consistently I do them, the more meaningful my leadership will be. So, everything else I believe in and practice as a leader needs to fit with that philosophy.

My framework for leadership is drawn from multiple sources and covers three big ideas: One, what leaders and managers do, which I base mostly on the works of John Kotter. Two, the key capabilities of great leaders, which I base mostly on a *Harvard Business Review* article titled "In Praise of the Incomplete Leader." And, three, the key application areas for leading innovation and change, which I base mostly on the concepts in *The Start-up J-Curve* by Howard Love. While many other ideas help shape my framework, those three provide a good summary and come into play daily as I serve as a dean.

I'll give you an overview of all three, then use the rest of the book to illustrate how I've put that framework in practice as dean of the Walton College.

Complexity and Change: What Leaders Do

It seems pretty obvious these days that leadership and management are different but complementary animals. However, the idea was pretty novel and actually sparked some debate in 1977 when Abraham Zaleznik questioned the differences in an article for *Harvard Business Review* (Zaleznik 1977). Kotter would later break down the differences in a seminal *HBR* article, "What Leaders Really Do" (Kotter 1990), and subsequent book *John P. Kotter on What Leaders Really Do* (Kotter 1999). His take on leadership and management provides a starting point for my framework.

Kotter began with the premise that management is about "coping with complexity," while leadership is about "coping with change" (Kotter 1990). Then he highlighted the differences by looking at three ways they play out in normal organizational settings:

- Managers plan and budget, while leaders set direction.
- Managers organize and staff, while leaders align people to a shared vision.
- Managers provide control and solve problems, while leaders motivate and inspire.

There's much more to it, of course, or else he never would have gotten an entire *HBR* article out of his ideas, much less a book. But those simplified distinctions are easy to remember and therefore easy to put into practice in meaningful ways.

The role of a business school dean skews heavily toward leadership—helping others deal with the inevitable rapid changes of their world. That's why I believe my role primarily revolves around setting direction for the college, gaining alignment on a shared vision, and motivating others to overcome the obstacles that come as the result of change. To do that, however, I often find myself needing to manage effectively—I have to bring order and predictability to complex environments.

The trick is to manage when the situation calls for management and lead when the situation calls for leadership. That's not always easy, but it's close to impossible if you don't know the differences between the two animals. When you know what leaders and managers actually do, on the other hand, you can go about the business of doing those things with intentionality, and that consistently leads to more positive results.

Incompleteness: The Capabilities of Great Leaders

When I referenced my leadership philosophy earlier, I pointed out that I am not perfect. It seems so obvious as to hardly be worth mentioning, but I mention it again because I recognize the very real temptations leaders face to deny or hide our imperfections. The sooner we embrace that it's OK to admit we're not perfect and we all need help, the sooner we can find that help and lead more collaboratively and effectively.

That's why I appreciate the approach Deborah Ancona, Thomas W. Malone, Wanda J. Orlikowski, and Peter M. Senge took a few years ago in their *HBR* article, "In Praise of the Incomplete Leader" (Ancona et al. 2007). It starts with the idea that no leader is flawless, so the best leaders accept their strengths and weaknesses, and then find others who complement them by making up for their weaknesses and bolstering their strengths.

The authors contend that effective leadership involves four capabilities—sensemaking, relating, visioning, and inventing—so leaders need to understand those, develop them, use them, and lean into others who have them. Here's how they summarize those capabilities:

Sensemaking—Constantly understanding changes in the business environment and interpreting their ramifications for your industry and company.

Relating—Building trusting relationships, balancing advocacy (explaining your viewpoints) with inquiry (listening to understand others' viewpoints), and cultivating networks of supportive confidants.

Visioning—Creating credible and compelling images of a desired future that people in the organization want to build together.

Inventing—Coming up with new ways of approaching tasks or overcoming seemingly insurmountable problems to turn visions into reality.

I'm fortunate to be surrounded by associate deans, assistant deans, department heads, and other leaders who bring those four capabilities to our team. Knowing their strengths in these areas helps me assign tasks, put together teams, and delegate or seek help to ensure my weaknesses don't slow us down.

The fact that no leader is flawless in all four areas, however, is not an excuse to permanently surrender one or more areas to others. I've made it a point, especially since becoming dean, to develop all four of those capabilities. By working to improve them, I not only grow my personal leadership abilities, but I'm also more aware of my gaps and, therefore, better able to see how other leaders on my team can help fill in those gaps. I'm constantly asking myself and others how well I'm doing with the four capabilities. I'm also constantly evaluating situations to determine which of the capabilities are needed for me and my team to lead more effectively.

In addition to getting team input, I lean into my formal and informal advisors. The informal advisors include virtually everyone who speaks into my life—my family, students, business leaders, academics and administrators at other universities, and on and on the list goes. The formal advisors include my mentors, my Dean's Alumni Advisory Council, my Dean's Executive Advisory Board, and my Dean's Roundtable of Entrepreneurs and Market Makers. Those last three groups, in particular, provide invaluable input for the direction we take with the college, as well as for my personal leadership growth.

Of the four capabilities, my greatest strength is in relating. In many cases, I've been through the exact situations faced by the people I now lead. I know what it's like to be a student, faculty member, department chair, associate dean, business owner, and so on. I truly can empathize with them. Even if I haven't gone through the exact experiences, chances are I've gone through something similar and relate to it in some way that helps me appreciate the problems of those I lead and work with them on solutions.

I have found that relating well to others begins by not jumping to conclusions about who they are, what they think, what they are doing, or what they are going through in life. You never know what someone is experiencing. You don't know if they are going through a divorce or they've just been diagnosed with cancer or they are dealing with taking care of their aging parents or their kid is on opioids. You just don't know.

I feel like it's my responsibility to encourage people and build them up, regardless of whether I like them or agree with them and regardless of whether they are struggling or everything is going well. They are infinitely valuable, and I need to view them that way. When I do, I find it much easier to find common ground.

In hindsight, I think it's one of the reasons I'm in my position and have done well. I don't think I'm the most talented person in the world, and I've said plenty of things people don't like. But people trust me in part because I relate well to them. If someone trusts you, then they want you to lead. They don't have to worry about what you might do. People know that I care about them and that I care about the people around them. They trust that I'll do my best to do what's right for them and the college.

This commitment often shows up in how I coach many people in my organization. I ask each of them a similar question: *Where do you want to go and how can I help you get there?* I ask about their short-, medium-, and long-term goals. The answers allow me to relate to them and make decisions that help them achieve their goals.

For instance, one leader told me he wanted to move up to a better-paying job with more responsibility, but he didn't feel like his current job was preparing him for such a promotion. So I found ways to expand his duties to include more involvement with strategic thinking. Another direct report told me she wanted to stay in her position but improve some of the skills she needed to excel in her work. So I looked for new assignments that would challenge her to learn and practice the types of skills she wanted to improve.

In both cases, I could find ways to relate to what those employees wanted and then take action to serve them as a leader.

There's a natural tendency for deans to be pulled toward those in power—sort of like responding to a gravitational force that emanates from wealthy donors, influential faculty members, and high-level administrators. But I'm convinced it's equally important to love and care for all the many other people who support me in my role or who need my support as dean, from administrative assistants to direct reports to students.

The students, the very lifeblood of any university and its colleges, often get forgotten the higher an administrator moves up the org chart. Thankfully, my natural focus is on students. I've been blessed with four children, as well as nieces and nephews, and several of them have attended the University of Arkansas.

They serve as a reminder of the importance of relating to students' needs so that our work can transform their lives. I don't like to hear about faculty mistreating students in any way, because it has always upset me when I've felt like teachers (in high school) or faculty members (in college) were mistreating my own family members. I've been a bulldog when it comes to creating a culture that cares for our students, and I believe our faculty are well aware of this.

Keeping in tune with this culture is a simple matter of listening to our students. I still teach one class each year, so naturally I interact with those students. In 2019, we formed a Dean's Student Collaboration Team—a group of students who provide their perspective on how we can better implement our mission and live our core values as a college. When I invited this group to our executive committee meeting in December 2019, they came with five different big ideas, including an analysis of strengths, weaknesses, opportunities, and threats for each idea.

I also make a point to talk to students when I pass them in the hall, as I walk from my parking spot to my office each day, during events the college hosts, or anywhere else our paths might cross. (I'll talk more about proactive listening in a later chapter.)

This emphasis on students is a part of our values as a college. If we take care of our students, then we are catalysts for transforming their lives. So I'm always thinking about what we can do as an organization to achieve that. For example, we reorganized part of the college—putting one person in charge of the administrative functions that support students, from recruitment to placement—because we felt it was a better way to serve students.

We've also formalized our "relating" process by increasing the use of metrics to track how well we're serving all of our stakeholders. When I became dean, I sat down with my associate deans and asked, *How satisfied are our students? Do they think we're doing a good job? How satisfied are recruiters with our business school? How satisfied are parents when they come for orientation or for tours? How satisfied are our alumni?* I couldn't get solid answers to any of those questions. Nobody knew. So one of my goals was to change that, and now we conduct surveys and use tools like the Net Promoter Score to gather and analyze data that tells us not only how we're perceived but also, when we dig deeper, what causes those perceptions.

It's one of the many ways we use metrics to measure our organizational health and to assess how well we're living up to our mission, vision, and values.[3]

Most recently, we've created a task force to examine how well we're doing with the quality of our relationships with students. This idea was the direct result of an article I read in early 2019 by *New York Times* columnist David Brooks. He points out that neuroscience is confirming the importance in education of a positive relationship between teachers and students. The research reminds us, he wrote, "that children learn from people they love, and that love in this context means willing the good of another, and offering active care for the whole person." He added, "The bottom line is this, a defining question for any school or company is: What is the quality of the emotional relationships here?" (Brooks 2019).

The task force we created will help us evaluate how well we can measure our answers to that question and take steps to improve relationships in ways that deepen learning and truly transform students' lives.

Putting the *How* and *What* Together

As you can see, Kotter addresses the "what" of leadership, while Ancona *et al.* cover the "how." Each model is insightful on its own merits, but they are even more powerful when integrated. Table 4.1 illustrates how these frameworks complement one another and provides a glimpse into why they are such a significant part of my approach to leadership. You can use

---

3. I will share much more about our marketing efforts and our metrics in subsequent chapters.

		WHAT LEADERS DO		
		Setting Direction	**Gaining Alignment**	**Providing Motivation**
HOW LEADERS LEAD	Sensemaking	Leaders who clearly explain how phenomena in their industries are impacting their organizations provide credibility to the direction that they have set.	Clearly articulating changes in the industry and their impact helps employees see the value in joining forces. This is especially true when there is a common threat.	Understanding where an industry is going and how that affects an organization serves as a catalyst for employees to move in the right direction.
	Relating	The art of conversation ensures clarity when setting direction. Conversation also creates an environment of procedural justice for the direction that is set.	Relating to others facilitates the networking within an organization that is necessary for gaining alignment.	People are more motivated to help leaders they trust, and trust is built on strong relationships of mutual understanding and respect.
	Visioning	Creating a mental image of the direction makes it more credible and easier to remember.	A well-illustrated mental model helps everyone "see" the organization's future and, therefore, makes it more likely that they will go in the same direction.	Appealing mental images inspire people to action.
	Inventing	Obstacles always exist to a worthwhile direction. When the leaders and their teams co-invent solutions, it clarifies and adds specificity to the direction, while creating additional procedural justice in the process.	Gaining alignment is a significant obstacle to moving in a particular direction. Leaders with a strong inventing capability have an advantage because they can invent mechanisms to align the organization.	It takes creativity and innovation to come up with effective incentives to motivate the organization.

Table 4.1. Integrating the *What* and *How* of Leadership

the table to make sure you don't miss any of the key cells of the intersection between the what and the how of leadership. (Appendix C is a blank version of the framework that you can copy and fill out as you apply it to specific projects.)

The value of effective sensemaking is most noticed when it is absent. If an organization doesn't understand a key part of the reason for moving in a particular direction, then employees aren't aligned and motivated. People want to know why they are doing something or not doing something, especially when it has to do with the strategic direction of the organization. In my experience, more than one person must be involved in the process of creating a well-conceived sensemaking narrative, and the narrative itself will be refined over time. New information will be interpreted, and the sensemaking narrative will pivot.

Every Monday morning we have a meeting of the Dean Team—me, Anne O'Leary-Kelly, Alan Ellstrand, and Brent Williams—and a lot of sensemaking goes on quite naturally during those sessions. I'm sure some people are more prone to engage in sensemaking than others, but I also believe that sensemaking is heavily affected by team chemistry. Our team has great sensemaking chemistry. In addition to our weekly meeting, the Dean Team meets for an extended lunch once per month and extensive sensemaking goes on during that lunch.[4]

The relating capability also helps with setting direction, not only because it creates alignment and motivation but also because it helps determine the direction. As conversations unfold between the leadership team and key constituents, pivoting occurs in regard to the direction of the organization. If directions are not tweaked, they will not be as effective because

---

4. I actually have a recording of an extemporaneous sensemaking session. The first podcast I ever recorded was a sensemaking session with the Dean Team. During our lunch, I pulled out the equipment and proposed recording a podcast of us engaging in sensemaking. They very reluctantly agreed. Here it is: https://walton.uark.edu/be-epic-podcast/the-dean-team.php. I must say that I'm a little embarrassed to share it due to the lack of planning and sound quality but I think it gives a great example. One other example is a virtual meeting the four of us had and recorded for the college during the COVID-19 crisis. Here is the video: https://www.linkedin.com/posts /mattwallerphd_covid19-crisismanagement-crisiscommunication-activity -6646760246851223552-rreB.

of uncertainty and equivocality in the information at any point in time. Ongoing conversations reduce the uncertainty and resolve the equivocality. Simply sharing information in emails is not sufficient for equivocality reduction.[5] This conversation also drives procedural justice, which enhances alignment and motivation.[6]

Visioning is one of the more obvious capabilities of leaders. Again, however, it usually takes more than one person to create a mental image for the organization that is well-illustrated, appealing, and inspirational. In fact, the ongoing sensemaking and relating also help to create a compelling vision. In my opinion, consistent work at sensemaking and relating, especially when pivoting, will result in a winning vision.

Inventing is a capability that clears obstacles to the direction, creates compelling processes to alignment, and comes up with incentive mechanisms for motivation. Again, hard work, effort, and time in sensemaking, relating, and visioning will make the inventing come about naturally. So for all of this to work, lots of effort must go into sensemaking and relating, in part because they set the stage for collaboration.

Riding the Curve: Leading Innovation and Change

My office sits on land once owned by William McIlroy, who migrated from North Carolina to Arkansas as a young man and had success as a farmer and merchant before co-founding one of the state's first banks.

In 1871, McIlroy sold 160 acres of his hilltop farm to the state of Arkansas as a location for the Arkansas Industrial University. The first classes at what would later become known as the University of Arkansas took place in January 1872 with seven students—six male and one female. The business college was founded in 1926, and it grew steadily for the next seven

---

5. For more on this, see "Organizational Information Requirements, Media Richness and Structural Design" by Richard L. Daft and Robert H. Lengel, Management Science, Vol. 32, No. 5, Organization Design (May 1986), pp. 554–571, available at https://www.jstor.org/stable/2631846, last accessed 17 December 2018.

6. I'll discuss procedural justice in more detail later in the book; for now, it's important to know I'm talking about how getting people involved in processes and decisions applies in organizational dynamics.

decades. Then the Walton Family Charitable Support Foundation made a watershed donation of $50 million to the college in 1998. It was renamed the Sam M. Walton College of Business Administration in honor of the founder of Walmart, and the official name was shortened in 2000 to the Sam M. Walton College of Business.

What all that background tells you is that the Walton College, much like the business colleges at many major universities, is well along in years. That means I lead and manage a mature organization with some policies and procedures that have been in place for decades. And yet, this institution thrives largely due to an incredible amount of entrepreneurial efforts. The student body is constantly turning over, with freshmen and new graduate students arriving every year. Those students and the faculty are committed not only to studying theories based on what's happened in the past but also to adding to and developing new theories and best practices that will change the future.

A dean's leadership and management framework must account for this dynamic element, and mine does so primarily by filtering initiatives through a J-curve diagram.

A J-curve graph tracks something that typically has an initial fall followed by a steep rise and that finishes above its starting point. It's most commonly used in economics, medicine, and political science. Ian Bremmer deserves credit for bringing the term more mainstream with his 2006 book *The J Curve: A New Way to Understand Why Nations Rise and Fall*. He uses the x-axis to plot the openness of (or freedom) of a nation, while the y-axis plots the stability. A closed government (like China or Cuba) is very stable. Stability decreases initially when governments allow more freedom and openness. Eventually, however, a more free and open society (like the United States) stabilizes until it is far more stable than the closed system.

In some ways, the Walton College is like a mini-nation, so Bremmer's theories apply. Our goal as a college is to maintain stability through openness with our stakeholders. But I have another reason for using this model. The college also is like an ever-evolving start-up that's constantly reinventing itself, and that's what led me to lean so heavily on another version of the J-curve.

Howard Love, who has founded or cofounded fifteen companies, tweaked Bremmer's idea and created a model that applies to entrepreneurship, which he outlines in *The Start-up J-Curve* (Love 2016). Love points out that start-ups typically grow through six phases that form a J-curve rather than an upward diagonal line on a graph (Love 2016). We consistently launch new initiatives within the Walton College, and I treat them like start-ups by leading and managing our team through those same six stages. Viewing it through this lens helps me understand and respond to the people and processes regardless of which stage they are in.

Take a closer look at the stages:

Create—In the create phase, I'm trying to come up with the idea, team, and resources. Sometimes it's my idea, but usually it comes from others. If it fits with our values and serves our mission and vision, then it is worth considering. If as a team we decide to pursue it, then I start by saying something like, "Here's what I think is the idea. Do I understand this correctly? Let's put together a team to reduce this idea to something that can be put into practice. How are we going to do this?"

The resources involve funding the idea. As the leader of the college, it's my responsibility to make sure we have the resources, whether that's from internal sources or externally through for-profit programs—revenue-generating programs or philanthropy. But the buck stops with me. If I get an initiative going and can't raise the funds, the failure is completely my fault and I take responsibility for it. I make this clear to everyone up front, which takes the burden off them, because people sometimes think, *If I start this and then I can't get it going, it's going to make me look bad.* I relieve them of that burden by saying, "I am responsible for the resources." Everyone else then feels free to move forward. This also is a good way for me to assess how confident and committed I am to the idea. I have to be very confident and committed to move forward with such a significant responsibility.

So from the start of the innovation, I've set a clear vision and direction. I have related to their pain points about executing that vision, and I have helped make sense of where we're going, why, and how we're going to get there. This creates alignment and provides motivation. Every element of my framework has come into play, and each one matters as we work our way through the other phases.

Release—Once an initiative is created, there comes a time when it's ready to launch. Often, this takes a toll on the team and the budget, and it inevitably arrives with a few disappointments and failures.

That's why the line on a graph dips down to create the bottom curve in a J.

Morph—The release leads to a regrouping as the team figures out what worked, what didn't work, and how best to reshape the initiative into the best possible version of itself.

Model—Once the kinks are worked out, the business model—and this is important even in an academic environment—needs to be perfected. The best initiatives add value to the college by clearly helping us reach our stated goals in a financially responsible way.

Scale—Now the initiative is in a position to grow, which brings about excitement but also new challenges. The initiative may scale to include other colleges within the university, more outside business partners, or to have an influence on universities and/or businesses in new geographic regions.

Harvest—Once the initiative has proven itself, it becomes an established program and you can lead and manage it with that mindset.

Again, my leadership framework provides a guide for shepherding the innovation through each phase. The vision and direction for the initiative might stay the same throughout, but it might change because innovation almost always brings unexpected challenges and opportunities. The key is to make sure that, regardless of any changes, it still aligns with your overall mandate as it progresses through every phase in the curve. The leader must strengthen the alignment and, in some cases, expand it to new stakeholders. And the leader must continually motivate, especially when things are going well. All of this requires sensemaking, relating, visioning, and inventing.

PART III

The 12-Lane Highway

Leading a business college often feels like driving down a crowded inter-state highway with unmarked exits. Everything around you demands your attention, and one wrong move could send you into a ditch or down some backroad to nowhere. This final section goes into specifics about some of the lanes you'll find yourself in, from leading large change initiatives to expressing gratitude, so that you can navigate them more successfully.

CHAPTER 5

Activating Change

The framework I've outlined leans heavily toward leading an organization into and through change. That's partly because that's what all leaders do—cope with change, as Kotter put it. This imperative, however, is even more relevant, I believe, when it comes to leading a modern business college.

For starters, business colleges are in the change business. The best colleges research what has changed in business, study what is changing, and prepare students for the present realities and for what's to come.

There are principles and theories of business that seldom change (if at all) over time. But disruptions—whether they come from new technologies or unforeseeable circumstances like the coronavirus pandemic—are changing how those principles apply. They change how people work, what customers want, how products and services are delivered, and even how people think about business, products, services, and each other. What we know (and teach) about marketing, management, accounting, economics, finance, information systems, supply chain, entrepreneurship, and the like, is very different today than it was even five years ago, and it will be very different five years from now.

Business colleges operate in and are shaped by this unprecedented environment of change. They are in no way immune to the broader climates of change in the world; indeed, they are experiencing specific and significant shifts as a subset of the education industry. Technology, primarily trends in online education, are disrupting higher education in ways unseen since the invention of the printing press. That means deans of business colleges have to embrace risks and lead change, not just teach change.

Near the end of the summer of 2019, our chancellor held an offsite strategic planning meeting that included the provosts, vice-chancellors, and deans. We split into groups, and each group took a different trend in higher education and tried to answer the question, "What would the university look like if this particular trend were carried out to its logical conclusion?" It was challenging for all the groups. Some members focused on why they thought things wouldn't happen rather than on what could or should be done in a future that looks different from what they might expect.

I want the Walton College to help create the future of higher education, not just respond to it. And I believe every dean of every business college should prioritize innovation and entrepreneurship in some form.

This is the lifeblood of business. And when you think about it, it's the lifeblood of a business college. A business that isn't innovative and entrepreneurial soon goes out of business, but an even worse fate awaits a business college that takes a status quo approach. Rather than dying off, it typically hangs around on life-support but becomes irrelevant.

Simply put, if the dean of a business college isn't proactively leading change, then that dean is destined to struggle and likely to underperform.

Business colleges need to model innovation by practicing what we preach, so to speak, and by creating the future that other colleges can emulate. In my tenure as dean of the Walton College, for instance, we have expanded our distance-learning offerings, created an executive education satellite campus in Little Rock, Arkansas, spun off a new department that focuses on entrepreneurship and innovation, added seven new master's degree options, and launched a massive overhaul of our on-campus MBA program.

The two biggest and most challenging changes by far were the overhaul of the MBA program and the creation of a new department. Those case studies provide some insights into how my framework has helped me play my part in activating change at the Walton College.

Repeating History

When Dan Worrell envisioned a stand-alone Department of Supply Change Management at the Walton College, he dipped into his personal expertise in change management to help make it happen. I learned a great deal from him during that time period about leading change, and those lessons align with and complement my framework. I have leaned heavily on those lessons as dean, but never more so than when I decided the Walton College needed a Department of Strategy, Entrepreneurship and Venture Innovation (SEVI).

This decision, interestingly enough, has its roots in my commitment to our mandate. I constantly think about our mission. I do this to critically evaluate both the mission itself and how well we're living it out. Entrepreneurship is one of the primary strategic endeavors where we're supposed to encourage innovation, but I found myself questioning whether we were really doing that and if doing it really mattered.

That last question—Does it really matter?—stuck with me like gum on a shoe. I didn't have an immediate answer, and it seemed crazy that I could be the dean of a business school with entrepreneurship in the mission statement and not be able to articulate why that part of our mission made sense or defend an objection to it.

I've had business leaders tell me that entrepreneurs don't need a college degree. To some extent, that's true. A lot of very successful entrepreneurs were college dropouts. Are people like Steve Jobs, Mark Zuckerberg, and Richard Branson the exception that proves the rule, I wondered, or are entrepreneurs actually better off when they don't spend time or money on a business degree?

So that's where I started: Does a business degree really help an entrepreneur? Or could all the things we're already doing to promote and aid entrepreneurship really go on without a connection to a business college?

I thought about those questions and discussed them with faculty and students who were going through or had gone through our undergraduate and master's programs. Along the way, I did some research on the founders of successful companies. Of the top fifty companies on the Fortune 500 list, for instance, forty-three had easily identifiable founders. The others were founded by the US government (Fannie Mae and Freddie Mac) or were formed by so many mergers and acquisitions that it was difficult to designate a founder or co-founders (Citigroup, Marathon Petroleum, Anthem, IBM, and MetLife). Several went back to the 1800s and a few even further.

In many cases, the education records for the founders were unclear. But of those forty-three companies, I found that at least twenty-five had a founder who had earned a college degree, including at least nine with a founder who had earned a degree in business. And four others had at least one founder who had spent some time studying business in college.

Some notable founders with an undergraduate in business or an MBA include Sam Walton (Walmart), Stanley Goldstein (CVS), Robert Walter (Cardinal Health), Charles Walgreen (Walgreens), Ralph Roberts (Comcast), Dan Duncan (Enterprise Products), and Sandy Lerner (Cisco).

John D. Rockefeller (Standard Oil, now ExxonMobil) and Henry Ford (Ford Motor), meanwhile, both took college bookkeeping courses before launching their business careers.

I also found that many of the world's top companies were born from ideas that originated with college work, regardless of whether the founder earned a degree.

Mark Zuckerberg started Facebook while at Harvard. He completed his initial platform using Harvard students and later expanded it to nearby universities such as MIT. Before Trip Hawkins earned his MBA at Stanford, he created his own major at Harvard in strategy and applied game theory. From that he came up with the idea behind Electronic Arts, the highly successful video game publishing company. Urban Outfitters, founded by Richard Hayne, Judy Wicks, and Scott Belair, was based on a group project for a class on entrepreneurship at the University of Pennsylvania's Wharton School. Nike was partly based on a paper that co-founder Phil Knight wrote while earning his MBA at Stanford. And Fred Smith launched FedEx based on a paper he wrote as a student at Yale.

To get a better feel for more current founders, I decided to look at the Inc. 5000. It ranks private companies in the United States based on five-year growth, so it provides a glimpse into entrepreneurial founders who are on the rise. I looked at the founders of twenty-five companies—the top ten on the 2018 Inc. 5000, the top ten on the 2019 Inc. 5000, and the five in 2019 that had made the list for fourteen straight years. Of the thirty-one founders/co-founders of those companies, I could confirm that at least twenty-eight had earned a bachelor's degree or higher in some field and at least twenty-two had earned a degree of some type in business.

None of that research definitively proved that a business degree adds value to an entrepreneur, however. So next, I took a step in deductive reasoning by brainstorming and vetting reasons a business degree helps an entrepreneur succeed.

My first thought was, *Well, if you're going into business then you really need to know how to read financial statements, so you need accounting and finance. And you need to understand business law.* Eventually, I had twenty-eight reasons. Then I condensed that list into nine primary areas: finances, business planning, business execution, sales and marketing, legal issues, technology, human resources, networking, and leadership.

It was also around this time that I formed a board that would advise me on strategic matters associated with how entrepreneurship would advance the mission of the college. I sent invitations to all of the entrepreneurs I knew, most of them alumni, thinking that about twenty percent would agree to help. All but one agreed. All of a sudden I had a third board, and it was large—about sixty members!

I was going to call them the Dean's Advisory Board of Entrepreneurs and Leaders, or DABEL (pronounced "dabble"). I sent a group email to them proposing that name, and it only took about one minute for me to get a response from a very creative entrepreneur, Sean Womack.

"Entrepreneurs don't dabble," he said. "You need a new name: DREAM—Dean's Roundtable of Entrepreneurs and Market-Makers."

I loved the name. But more than that, I loved the insights this DREAM team has given me around the importance of a business college to a thriving entrepreneurial community. I was reminded, for instance, that the Walton College produces talent that fills the labor pools for existing start-up companies, while also preparing would-be entrepreneurs to launch their own ventures.

Ultimately, I was convinced that a business degree helps entrepreneurs. It's not a necessary condition, but it can increase their probability of success. Entrepreneurship involves taking risks, but it also involves a certain set of skills for navigating in the business world. I confirmed my intuitive belief that having an education from a good business school provides a fundamental base of knowledge that enhances an entrepreneur's opportunities for success.

While there's a financial price for a college education, it's not as high as the tuition at the School of Hard Knocks. A degree in business helps entrepreneurs make fewer mistakes on the front end, learn more quickly from the mistakes they can't avoid, have a better understanding of the path they are forging, and know how to hire the right experts to complement their needs. It puts them in a position to grow their company or initiative for the long haul.

This conclusion led me to another question. If entrepreneurs need a business degree and we were supposed to encourage innovation in entrepreneurship, then maybe we should do even more to support this part of our mission. That's when we really began to explore the merits of forming a new department. I found myself squarely in the "create" phase of the J-curve.

At the time, the Management Department at the Walton College included faculty and programs in Organizational Behavior/Human Resource Management (OB/HRM) and in Innovation, Entrepreneurship and Strategic Management (IESM). After I met with administrators, faculty, and business leaders across our community, I was convinced we needed to reorganize the Department of Management into two departments so that each could reach its full potential. One of those meetings, of course, was with Dan Worrell, the former dean who was serving as interim chair of the management department. He believed it was a good move and encouraged me to make it.

All of that research and all of those meetings, in other words, helped me set a new direction, and it equipped me with the information I need to align people around the vision and to motivate and inspire the change.

As we did when creating the supply chain department, we gathered letters from business leaders and made a strong case for needing to make this move. And in March 2019, I sent an email to our faculty and staff laying out the benefits of the change. The state, for instance, would benefit from a new generation of entrepreneurs, and we needed to do our part to nurture new venture developments. We must develop strong entrepreneurship-focused curricula, innovation experiences for students and young entrepreneurs, and cross-sector partnerships, and we must be agile in our teaching and research initiatives.

While our existing management department gained a strong statewide and international reputation in entrepreneurship through the success of our outstanding business plan teams and subsequent startup companies, our success in innovation and entrepreneurship had been limited to a few areas. Plus, we had not fulfilled our potential to make a broader contribution to economic development in the state. A distinct department, composed of faculty with expertise in innovation, entrepreneurship, and strategic management, I said, would prepare future entrepreneurs to identify innovation opportunities. It would also enable them to understand increasingly fluid organizational structures and dynamic business environments.

In addition, the new department would be perfectly positioned to benefit from and create benefits from the investments that the college and university already had made in innovation and entrepreneurship, including the Brewer Family Entrepreneurship Hub and the McMillon Innovation Studio. It would provide much-needed faculty depth in these areas—particularly in staffing our MBA entrepreneurship classes, which relied heavily on the expertise of one faculty member and therefore were not scalable.

Establishing the new SEVI Department was consistent with the emphasis on innovation and entrepreneurship in the Walton College strategic plan while also supporting the chancellor's priority of building an innovative and collaborative campus. The inherently interdisciplinary nature of SEVI would enable it to effectively partner with other departments in the college and across campus. The department would be well-positioned to act as a bridge to connect technical expertise in other colleges with business knowledge in the Walton College. These efforts would support the growth of interdisciplinary programs and research as well as commercialization efforts on campus.

The new department also would benefit students, faculty, and programs. The management major is general by design and does not enable students to gain deep knowledge in any particular area. Innovation and entrepreneurship faculty share a common interest with strategic management faculty when it comes to innovation and competitive advantage. Thus, a distinct department would provide an agile platform for the interdisciplinary, cross-sector approach that is necessary to innovative program offerings.

Students and faculty in the new department can engage with the local start-up ecosystem, providing unique practice-based learning and research experiences. This inimitable environment provides the foundation for growing the national reputation of the new department. Building a strong program in these areas would enable us to transform the lives of many more students (undergraduate and graduate) and provide a more focused field for faculty collaboration and research.

MBA Overhaul

The Walton College full-time MBA program ranked among the top forty public business schools in America in 2019, according to *US News and World Report*, so you might wonder why we would fix what didn't appear to be broken. Indeed, we didn't see it as broken. But after extensive feedback from employers and alumni, as well as researching the MBA market, we realized that "strong" had to become much stronger for us to stay competitive and serve our mission. The time to innovate was now.

Full-time MBA programs often operate at a deficit these days. The costs of running quality programs continues to rise, while enrollments decline, partly because of an increased interest in online programs. Several top business colleges, in fact, have dropped their full-time MBA. Geis Business College at the University of Illinois, for instance, was a top-fifty program, but enrollment in its full-time MBA class had fallen from 386 in 2016 to 290 in 2019 when it announced it was moving exclusively to an online approach. The University of Iowa, Wake Forest University, and Virginia Tech University are among the other major schools that have dropped the full-time MBA option (Byrne 2019).

To make a full-time MBA an attractive option for students, the program must reflect the changing needs of the labor market. The skills needed to succeed in business have morphed, so we needed to pivot to better meet the needs of our students and employers. To improve our offerings, we decided we needed to completely redesign the full-time MBA.

Most programs improve through iterative changes, but we needed break-through progress that would only come with some short-term pain. That pain would come from shutting down the program while we jumped into the "morph" phase and remodeled.

We had a choice—either have a hiatus or have two overlapping programs. We decided to take a hiatus. That meant we would not have an entering class for Fall 2018, which meant we would not have a graduating class three years down the road. And that meant we would fall completely out of the rankings, since stats like average GMAT scores and GPA of incoming students, placement rates for graduates, and average starting salaries of graduates all are part of the criteria. In short, the ranking of our program would take a hit for three years, but we expect it to climb quickly and dramatically beginning in 2021 after the first newly admitted cohort graduates.

We took this redesign risk because we felt it was the best way to improve the program in four key areas:

Content—We increased the track (concentration) depth by adding a fourth track, building the tacks around courses with experiential, real-world content, and emphasizing analytics. For instance, the marketing retail track now has a dedicated course in retail analytics.

Professional development—We improved and increased our expert workshops and certifications. For example, we added forty hours of training that leads to a certification on analytics. We also added an emphasis on negotiation skills, building a personal brand, and interviewing techniques.

Mentoring—We expanded our program that provides students with a corporate mentor who meets with them monthly. The mentoring committee of our MBA Alumni board also provides mentors who are "on call" to respond to issues students are facing.

Internships—Rather than just offering the traditional summer internships, we expanded our program so that students can intern for about twenty hours a week throughout the entire program. Vikas Anand, who at the time was the executive director of our MBA programs, pointed out that this helps both students and the companies that use them as interns.

"Organizations that know a student intern is going to be available for a length of time are willing to give them high levels of responsibility," Vikas wrote in a LinkedIn article about the changes. "The students get an opportunity to gain great work experience, to constantly apply classroom learning in the workplace, and incredible networking opportunities. Most such internships lead to permanent job offers and the augmented internship program was a big reason why the Walton MBA programs have had one of the best 'placement at graduation' rates in the country" (Anand 2019).

With these improvements to our already strong MBA program, we believe students will improve their skills in the core areas of disciplines like supply chain and marketing. And we believe they will graduate with an innovation mindset, learn from simulations and experiential projects, and develop strong partnerships with would-be employers.

The MBA program now is in the "model" stage. We closely monitor the progress and outcomes of these changes, benchmark and compare with multiple programs around the world, and conduct extensive surveys and interviews with alumni and corporate partners, as well as students and recruiters.

The work we're doing to create changes like adding a new department and revamping our MBA program are born of our belief that a business college can't meet the needs of the future if it stays mired in its past—no matter how wonderful that past has been. The world never stops changing, and business leaders are part of those changes—they create change and adapt to change on an ongoing basis.

I have to understand how to lead the changes we need to make so that we're meeting the needs of our students and the organizations they will lead once they graduate. My framework allows me to do that. I set the direction, cast the vision, align people around the vision, motivate them, help them make sense of the changes, relate to their struggles, help them come up with creative solutions to the barriers people face, and shepherd the initiatives through each phase in the J-curve.

CHAPTER 6

Institutionalizing Innovation

Starting a new department, creating the Blockchain Center of Excellence, and revamping our MBA program are three examples of ways the Walton College has taken risks and modeled innovation so that we're on the leading—or even bleeding—edge of our industry. But those types of bold actions don't happen without an entrepreneurial mindset that institutionalizes innovation throughout the culture.

Entrepreneurship and innovation both are mentioned in the Walton College mission, and innovation is the "I" in our EPIC values, so they are all key parts of our mandate. The sound of such words quickly fades, however, if there's no meaningful action behind them. We've been willing to innovate as a college in large part because we have a consistent, action-oriented focus on taking risks and creating disruptions that advance our mission. Because we've done this successfully with smaller opportunities, we've been prepared to do it on a larger scale.

The Walton College has a long history of researching, teaching, and practicing innovation. I see it as my duty to uphold that legacy by prioritizing this approach so that entrepreneurial best practices remain ingrained in our culture.

Here are some ways we have institutionalized innovation.

Sharing Our Innovation Narrative. Whenever and wherever we find opportunities, we try to tell others about the things we do that are innovative. You see that in our marketing efforts, of course, but you also should hear it in our classrooms, meetings, and other presentations.

In the 2019–20 school year, for instance, senior associate dean Anne O'Leary-Kelly came up with the idea of opening every meeting of the dean's executive committee with an "innovation talk" where a member takes five minutes to share and discuss a new best-practice or approach in his or her area.

In the first such talk, Supply Chain Management Chair Brian Fugate discussed his department's unique approach to internships. After two years of collecting data from meetings with students and the companies that hire students, the department created a plan that made internships a curriculum requirement. Then he and Kara Patterson began creating videos with students to capture and share their internship experiences. The videos are student-focused but also were a hit with the companies.

When we share our innovative best practices in the executive committee meetings, the other members can share the stories with their departments and incorporate ideas that might work for them. The stories also go into the meeting minutes, which are then shared with the entire college, reinforcing our commitment to innovation.

Practicing Continuous Improvement. Leaders don't drive change for the sake of change; they drive change that makes things better.

I'll talk more about strategic planning later, but one thing we emphasize in our planning is measuring the results. Why? So we can close the gaps where needed and iteratively improve on what we're already doing well. We want to get better at everything we're doing, so we focus on continuous improvement in every area of the college.

Our accreditation process, our marketing efforts, and our strategic planning help us drive continuous improvement.

If I do my job well, then the college is clear on our direction, aligned on our priorities, and motivated to create positive change that advances our mission.

At the start of the 2018 Fall semester, for example, we sent all the students in the college a link to a short questionnaire that, among other things, gave them the opportunity to share what they saw as our strengths and challenges. It resulted in a huge spreadsheet of information, and it led us to seek even more input. We did a similar survey of graduates at the end of the 2018–19 academic year. Then Vikas Anand, who at the time was faculty director of the Walton College MBA programs, went a step further by doing an exit interview with every graduate of the MBA and Executive MBA programs. It produced a wealth of insights, so now each member of my executive committee does five exit interviews with graduates each year, which garners us feedback from seventy-five students.

The point of collecting all this information is to use it to make us better. After getting the results of the first survey, I went to each member of the executive committee and asked them to review the results with a focus on the strengths and weaknesses relevant to their areas. Then I charged each of them with creating an action plan to close the loop in places where we need to improve. From a leadership perspective, I got alignment by allowing them to create the plans and provided motivation by tapping into their competitive nature.

One area where we've made what I believe will be game-changing improvements is with our student success initiatives. For instance, our first-year experience program, known as Freshman Business Connections, previously focused on giving new students all the resources they needed to be successful. While that sounds great, feedback from the students told us it wasn't effective. Many of our students felt that simply presenting opportunities and resources wasn't helpful because there were so many options.

Anne O'Leary-Kelly (senior associate dean), Karen Boston (assistant dean for student success), Jeff Hood (assistant dean and executive director for undergraduate programs), and Deb Williams (director of student programs for the Office of Entrepreneurship and Innovation) joined forces and reengineered the program. It now helps students answer a critical question: "Why are you here, and how can we help you design your Walton?"

The life-design approach was modeled off the Stanford Life Design experience, and it shifted the mindset of the class, not just the content. We also used feedback from employers, students, alumni, advisory boards, national standards, and our AACSB goals to create requirements and opportunities for students to meet milestones around key competencies. We call these SAMs (Students Achieving Milestones). Students can track their progress on an e-portfolio platform.

In Fall 2019, when we rolled out the changes, the class included sixty-four non-honors sections and had an enrollment of around 1,200 freshmen. The twenty-eight instructors included a cross-section of our faculty and staff.

Anne, Karen, Jeff, and Deb didn't just fix Freshman Business Connections. They exhibited thought leadership and created a totally new course that serves as a catalyst for transforming lives, which is the vision of the Walton College.

Interdisciplinary Innovation and Entrepreneurship. A university consists of many parts that can, and often do, operate independently of each other. But they all work together toward a common vision, and their individual missions at times can overlap. That's why it's important not to operate a business college in a vacuum. Working with other disciplines in a collaborative way accelerates innovation all across the campus.

Think about it: Entrepreneurs tap into the world around them—fields such as the sciences, technology, social needs, and the arts—and build new businesses around innovations that meet the needs they see. Yet, entrepreneurship at the university level often is taught only to students who are majoring in business.

The University of Arkansas is unique in that our approach to entrepreneurship is much more than a curriculum of classes that teach business theory and best practices to students who want a career in business. We've designed innovation and entrepreneurship programs that involve students from all across the campus and faculty from all across the campus and our community.

One example of this originated in 2017 when Alan Ellstrand and Karl Schubert met during our Walton Block Party, an annual event where faculty and staff mix with students. Ellstrand is the Walton College associate dean for academic programs and research, while Schubert holds a dual appointment in the Walton College and the College of Engineering.

Their conversation led to the creation of a combined class of around thirty freshmen engineering students and twenty Walton College students in the Honors Freshmen Business Connections program. The students work in teams for two semesters not only learning but developing solutions to real-world problems—everything from biodegradable glitter to a phone app that can unlock their rooms in the residence halls.

This type of interdisciplinary approach has become commonplace at the UA. In fact, the Walton College Office of Entrepreneurship and Innovation, which was established by Associate Vice-chancellor Carol Reeves and now is directed by Sarah Goforth, has worked with faculty and students from the College of Engineering, the College of Arts and Sciences, the College of Agriculture, and the School of Nursing.

One of our newer initiatives is the McMillon Innovation Studio, a physical space on campus where student-led teams collaborate on innovative projects. In 2018–19, the studio hosted a series of twenty innovation workshops teaching design thinking and agile and lean startup principles that attracted more than five hundred students. And forty-one students from twenty-one different majors were on design teams that worked on specific projects. At the end of the year, the teams showcased prototypes to more than seventy community members from corporations to startups. The interdisciplinary projects looked at . . .

- Using the ride-sharing concept for short shopping trips among friends and networks
- Giving customers assurance with online purchases so they are satisfied with the first shipment
- Helping people conveniently and quickly meal plan on a budget
- Alleviating mental stress for people with Type 1 diabetes
- Improving the on-the-road interactions between cars, trucks, and pedestrians

Our signature initiative, the New Venture Development Program, began in 2006 with a focus on combining business with the disciplines of science, technology, engineering, and math—STEM, as it's commonly known. The program offers a graduate certificate in entrepreneurship for non-business students who are working on a master's or PhD in a STEM field. The students take business classes and form project teams with our MBA students. And these teams have produced twenty-three high-growth startups businesses and won twenty-seven national competitions since 2009. They've won more than $3 million in prize money and raised more than $60 million in grants and equity.

The Office of Entrepreneurship and Innovation has been so successful that Sarah and her team decided to host our own startup competition. The Heartland Challenge, sponsored by the Walton Family Foundation, debuted in 2020, and more than one hundred student teams from around the world applied to compete for $135,000 in prize money.

We've also used the model developed by Reeves to create similar programs around social entrepreneurship and arts entrepreneurship.

Rogelio Garcia Contreras is the director of the Office of Social Innovation, which he founded in 2016 when he joined the UA faculty. The primary program is the Social Innovation Challenge, which creates interdisciplinary teams of students who partner with community organizations to help solve their pressing challenges by using entrepreneurial principles. More than 250 undergraduate students from multiple majors took part in the first two years of the program. They worked with more than twenty organizations on challenges ranging from food insecurity to homelessness to sustainable supply chains.

Adrienne Callander joined the UA in 2017 as professor of art and arts entrepreneurship at the University of Arkansas. She has a cross-appointment in the School of Art and the Walton College, so she not only teaches across disciplines but is building collaborative partnerships to generate entrepreneurship connected to the arts.

These diverse interdisciplinary programs all are supported by partnerships with community business leaders, and they extend well beyond the UA campus. In fact, we collaborate on events with other institutions around the state, including the University of Arkansas for Medical Sciences, the University of Arkansas at Little Rock, the University of Arkansas at Pine Bluff, and Arkansas State University. Reeves and her team have led seven multi-campus interdisciplinary faculty commercialization retreats and similar retreats for graduate and postdoctoral fellows.

All of these efforts put students in positions to learn about, and sometimes actually launch, new businesses, so they discover the phases of the J-curve not only in theory but also as they put theory into practice.

Student-led Entrepreneurship. ForeverRed looks and operates much like any other online business. It has around twenty-five workers in its accounting, commercialization, customer service, marketing, and operations departments. And it has succeeded by offering quality products at a fair price and by regularly exceeding its customers' expectations. The company is unique in several ways, however, not the least of which is that it begins each year with an entirely different staff. That's because it's a student-run enterprise that's part of the Walton College's SAKE program.

Reeves founded the Students Acquiring Knowledge through Enterprise (SAKE) Entrepreneurship Practicum in 1996 with the financial support of two Arkansas business legends, Frank Fletcher and Jerry Jones. Fletcher has built multiple successful companies, and his holding company has interests in auto dealerships, commercial real estate, a hotel, restaurants, and a retail store. Jones is a titan in the oil and gas industry but is perhaps best known as the owner of the Dallas Cowboys.

The Walton College offers an undergraduate and a graduate level class for students who want to take part in the SAKE practicum. The classes offer practical instruction from top faculty members and enable students to experience the joys and challenges of running a small business, developing new products, and working in a start-up organization. In other words, they experience the stages of the Start-up J-curve.

SAKE launched the ForeverRed brand in 2011. Its core business is the sale of framed student diploma sets that can include a rubbing of the student's name from the Senior Walk. It has expanded its product line in recent years to things like care packages for students and Hog Holograms.

ForeverRed is a nonprofit, but it operates on the same principles as a for-profit company. It broke even in FY 2016, but sales soared to $75,506 in FY 2017, a 35 percent increase that contributed to a net income of $12,074. Revenues rose again in FY 2018 (to $86,984) but net income fell to $3,934. Then revenue fell in FY 2019 (to $73,744) while net income jumped to $15,437.

What's more interesting than the numbers is the reasons behind them. Ali Sadeghi-Jourabchi, who oversees SAKE as an entrepreneur-in-residence, pointed out that the students changed to a new manufacturer in 2018 to reduce production time and create more control in their order processing. As a result, sales orders turned into recognized sales more quickly at the end of FY 2018, which meant there were fewer carry-over sales to start FY 2019.

"In FY 2019," Ali told me, "students generated lower cost of goods, higher profit margin and lower operational cost, hence better profitability."

In other words, they experienced firsthand how real business decisions affect real business outcomes.

In addition to learning about and operating a day-to-day business, the students often take on more long-range planning challenges. For instance, in 2018 eight students took part in a special summer session designed to address several key strategic issues, including improving financial tracking and reporting, the development of new marketing strategies, and the selection of new art prints for the expanding product portfolio.

SAKE also has been offering a spin-off class since Spring 2016, when it launched the SAKE Innovation Lab. Students in this class develop a business concept and assess the prospects of commercializing their idea. The first product developed by the class—the Freshman Survival Kit—includes school supplies, snacks and student-to-student advice on best practices for the transition to campus life. The product was sold to parents of entering freshmen during summer orientation in 2017 and delivered to students during the first week of classes. A similar product, the Finals Survival Kit, was marketed later in the fall semester. The Survival Kits have generated more than $7,500 in sales.

SAKE also started an internship program in Spring 2016. A contribution by Frank and Judy Fletcher subsidizes salaries so students can participate in paid internships at start-ups like BlueInGreen, Blogs for Brands, Grillight, and Menguin. Students also have worked with the University of Arkansas Bookstore to help develop its digital initiative.

Voices of Experience. One of the things that excites me the most about the future of the Walton College and our extended community is seeing our students interact with and learn from successful business leaders. That's why I love teaching honors courses—it's a chance to see students learn from the voices of experience, because I almost always include a variety of business leaders as guest speakers.

The topic of the course I taught in 2018 was entrepreneurship, and three or four Arkansas entrepreneurs joined us each week for the class. As pre-work, the students watched video interviews we had shot with the business leaders. After an in-class panel discussion with the entrepreneurs, each leader got with smaller groups of students to dive deeper into the joys and challenges of starting and running a business. Over the course of the semester, each student wrote LinkedIn articles about different entrepreneurs who had visited our class.

The Start-Up J Curve formed the course's backbone. Furthermore, the theories and principles of Love's book were richly illustrated by the entrepreneurs who interacted with the students. They got the valuable opportunity to hear talented men and women relate their experiences along the entrepreneurial cycle—their failures and disappointments, as well as their successes.

In some cases, the stories from our guests were playing out in real time. For instance, three of the entrepreneurs who spoke had major transactions during the semester. The day before Dan Sanker visited the class, he sold his company, Case Stack, for $255 million. As you might imagine, that experience made for some interesting discussion. Movista, Stan Zylowski's company, had just raised $12 million in venture capital on the evening he joined the class. And Blake Puryear's company, Engine, had recently raised $4 million in venture capital when he visited us.

The emphasis, however, was less about the success such leaders had achieved and more about the process that led to their achievements. In almost every case, the students learn that entrepreneurship is challenging and that there is pain associated with pivoting and morphing as a company finds its way forward along the curve described in Love's book. Knowing that process and the realities that come with following an entrepreneurial dream are essential in preparing students to prepare those dreams themselves.

Innovative Partnerships. For many business schools, partnerships with the corporate community look like using business leaders as guest lecturers, providing executive education to companies, asking companies to hire your graduates, and, of course, asking for financial donations. That's all great, but we also have found that partnering with innovative companies is a salient strategy for the success of a business school—and for the success of those companies.

My DREAM team—the Dean's Roundtable of Entrepreneurs and Market Makers—is a key part of this strategy. These men and women have proven helpful in a number of ways, from the insights they share to the solutions they provide.

During our first meeting, for instance, an issue came up regarding hiring our students. These entrepreneurial companies ranged from pre-revenue high-tech companies to growth companies, and our students often overlooked them at career fairs in favor of more established brands. Large companies, however, typically only hire students for internships during the summer before their senior year, so the DREAM companies agreed to hire interns earlier in their undergraduate journeys.

This solved a problem for the entrepreneurs. They got exposed to students earlier, so the students were less likely to overlook them later. In fact, the students were more likely to want to stay with them. Thus it gave the small entrepreneurial companies better access to young talent coming out of college. It solved a problem for college leadership, too, because we want more students in internships as soon as possible. We believe they learn more while they are in business school when they are working in substantial internships or co-ops. And it solved a problem for the students by providing them with more experience and better summer jobs. This was a win-win.

After the DREAM board formed, it struck me that it could serve the needs of the entire campus. So now the vice chancellor for economic development and the dean of the College of Engineering colead DREAM with me, which means they and their circles of influence also add to and get value from DREAM.

We also partner with larger companies, of course. Perhaps the best example of a next-level corporate partnership is our longstanding relationship with J.B. Hunt Transport Services, one of the most innovative and efficient logistics service providers in the United States.

If you think of J.B. Hunt as an old-school trucking company, you're missing out on one of the greatest stories of corporate innovation in US business history. It's a company that has grown over the years because, as former CEO and current chairman Kirk Thompson once put it, they "tolerate innovation" instead of getting lulled into a false sense of security because of their stellar record.

The spirit of innovation was evident in their founders, J.B. and Johnelle Hunt. It lives on in the company's current leadership team, which has helped refine a culture that understands how to press forward into a new future without sacrificing execution in the present. That's why JBHT has been able to build on its historic competencies like over-the-road trucking with innovative business models like intermodal services that partner with railroads, dedicated contract services (and final-mile delivery) that run the entire logistics operations for many companies, and integrated capacity solutions that provide high-end logistics brokerage services.

In 2017, JBHT announced a five-year, $500 million investment into "innovative and disruptive" technologies that, among other things, has helped create one of the most advanced logistics platforms available in the market. As Chief Information Officer Stuart Scott likes to put it, J.B. Hunt is no longer an assets company that uses technology; it's a technology company that uses assets.

The University of Arkansas is fortunate to have the headquarters of such an innovative company within a few miles of our campus—even more fortunate because many of J.B. Hunt's leaders are alumni. Thompson, who was inducted into the Arkansas Business Hall of Fame in 2018, began working at JBHT when he was still in college at the UA. Other Walton College graduates on the JBHT leadership team include John Roberts (president and CEO), Shelley Simpson (EVP, chief commercial officer and president of highway services), Nick Hobbs (president of DCS and final mile services), and Eric McGee (EVP of highway services).

J.B. Hunt's leaders have a long history of innovation, so it's no surprise that they've committed to innovative partnerships with the UA and the Walton College. Here are three examples:

- J.B. Hunt Supply Chain University Powered by Walton: In 2013, around three hundred JBHT sales executives from across the country attended the company's supply chain forum at the UA. It was so successful that the next year we partnered with the company to launch the J.B. Hunt Supply Chain University. Walton College faculty and J.B. Hunt executives collaborate on an innovative curriculum for J.B. Hunt employees that keeps them on the cutting edge of supply chain management.

- J.B. Hunt Innovation Center of Excellence: JBHT's $2.75 million research grant to the UA in 2017 marked the beginning of a new collaborative effort. The center brings together members of the UA College of Engineering, the Walton College, and the company's leaders. The interdisciplinary research that flows from the center allows engineering, computer science, and business researchers, and students to work with J.B. Hunt employees on innovative technology and design-driven solutions to supply chain challenges.

- J.B. Hunt On The Hill: Earlier this year, J.B. Hunt opened an office on the UA campus that will help Walton College students gain real-world experience in the transportation and logistics industry. J.B. Hunt On The Hill is housed in a 6,100-square-foot office suite at the Arkansas Research and Technology Park. It provides up to sixty interns per semester an opportunity to work in areas such as customer experience, engineering, and technology. The program includes guest lectures and workshops featuring J.B. Hunt leadership, clients, and vendors, as well as UA professors.

It's hard to find many companies that have made this type of investment in and on behalf of future leaders. But the leaders throughout JBHT are committed to the growth of their people, because they understand that those people will innovate business models and mechanisms that will keep the company ahead of its competition for decades to come. And while many Walton College students will go on to work for J.B. Hunt, many others will lead in other companies. So, JBHT's willingness to innovate stretches far beyond its walls and impacts the entire economy. That's visionary innovation at its finest.

Fostering Entrepreneurial Growth

Companies like J.B. Hunt, Walmart, Tyson Foods, DaySpring Cards, Sam's Club, Simmons Foods, George's, and Arc Best were founded within an hour's drive of the Walton College, and their success has created an entrepreneurial hunger in this region. In recent years, in fact, we've seen a new wave of start-ups launched by leaders who have emerged from existing companies or who have been inspired by them.

The Walton College, and, in fact, the entire University of Arkansas, plays a crucial role in this trend by providing students who are energized and prepared to take part. We can't play that role if we aren't innovative leaders ourselves. As dean of the Walton College, I am challenged to help find, create, and shepherd initiatives that support this part of our mandate. And I'm challenged to help create a culture that fosters entrepreneurial growth—inside the Walton College and all across our state.

You've already read about some of the ways we're doing that, but allow me to share one more.

The Brewer Family Entrepreneurship Hub opened in September 2017 on the square in historic downtown Fayetteville. It provides free meeting and coworking space for students and alumni, hosts events and workshops, and connects students to the entrepreneurial community. It holds office hours for experts in fields such as marketing, design, accounting, and law.

The hub is a joint resource for students in the New Venture Development program, the Social Entrepreneurship program, and the Arts Entrepreneurship program. It provides full-time office space to a variety of university groups, including faculty and staff from the Office of Entrepreneurship and Innovation; the student-run and managed Forever Red business; and STEAM-H, a program of the J. William Fulbright College of Arts and Sciences that bridges health care, engineering, design, science, and the arts.

The reason we're so committed at the UA to this interdisciplinary and collaborative approach to entrepreneurship is because, well, it works. We've seen the fruits. In fact, over the last year or so, I've invited a string of successful Arkansas-based entrepreneurs to sit down and share their stories. And one of the many things I've learned is that almost all of them have navigated the phases of Love's start-up J-curve. I have learned a lot from them about how to navigate those phases as the dean of the business college and, I hope, how to help their companies and the Walton College succeed over the long haul.

CHAPTER 7

Communicator in Chief

As the CEO of Procter & Gamble from 2000 to 2010 and again from 2013 to 2015, A. G. Lafley set a high standard for leadership success. He was known as a master of strategy who created a collaborative and innovative culture that pushed revenue through the roof. But what really separated him as a leader, according to many who worked with him, was his commitment to communication.

In *Playing to Win: How Strategy Really Works,* Lafley and coauthor Roger Martin say communicating strategy, internally and externally, is about answering five basic questions:

1. Who are we?
2. Where do we play?
3. How do we win?
4. What capabilities must be in place?
5. What management systems are required?

Those are great questions, but it's easy for leaders to get caught up in figuring out the answers and miss the important role of communication in the process. It's through communication that leaders find and share the answers to those types of questions so that the right things get done. Lafley was successful not only because he asked the right questions but also because communication was central to his leadership. In fact, Lafley once told Scott Mautz, who spent ten years as P&G's marketing director, that his job was "90 percent communication—communicating the next point especially" (Mautz 2019).

John Ryan, president of the Center for Creative Leadership and former superintendent of the US Naval Academy, calls communication "one of the most overlooked and undervalued of leadership skills" (Ryan 2009).

I couldn't agree more. That's why one of my roles as dean of the Walton College of Business is to serve as its communicator in chief.

I can outsource or delegate plenty of things, but I can never abdicate my responsibility for communication. Every leader on our team shares that responsibility, but no one more than myself. It's my responsibility, and I need to think about it every day. In fact, I believe that when you look at how a leader communicates you see a clear picture of how that leader actually leads—that is to say, how he or she uses sensemaking, relating, visioning, and inventing to set direction, align people to a shared vision, and motivate and inspire.

Communication isn't limited to the words we say or the messages we send in texts and emails. Communication also includes our actions, and our actions include our ability to listen effectively. Everything we say or do (or don't say or do) communicates a message to people who count on us for leadership. How we communicate and what we communicate are essential elements of effective leadership.

Two Ears, One Mouth

Before I focus on what I say or how I say it, I've found I need to tap into the leadership skill of "relating" by practicing effective listening. Lafley, like many truly great leaders, was known as a great listener—not only because he listened to his leadership team but also because he sought out and listened to everyone he could at every level, both inside and outside the organization. And he didn't just listen to hear, he listened to learn and understand.

"He met them in their homes and joined them on trips to the grocery store to better understand what they bought and why," said Ryan. "He made a point of getting out into the field to talk with colleagues. He knew that the best way to get good ideas was to ask for input and listen to it carefully" (Ryan 2009).

Stephen Covey's *The 7 Habits of Highly Effective People* outlines five types of listening:

1. Ignoring: To me, this is really just hearing as opposed to the skill of relating.
2. Pretending: I believe most people see straight through this disingenuous version of listening.

3. Selective hearing: This is tempting for me and many others, because we all have confirmation bias and tend to focus on the things that support our views.
4. Attentive: It takes effort and, in my experience, practice to lock eyes with someone and truly pay attention to what he or she is saying.
5. Empathic: This is where the skill of relating comes most into play, because it requires an ability to help other people know you genuinely care about how they feel about what they are saying.

Some key ways I've found for relating empathetically include making eye contact, taking notes, asking clarifying questions, and repeating what you've heard (what Covey calls "mimic" and "rephrase"). I've discovered that when I do those things, the atmosphere is almost always better.

I've understood the importance of listening for a long time, but the degree to which I apply it has grown significantly since I became dean. When I was named interim dean, for instance, I took some great advice from Chris Wyrick, who was vice chancellor for advancement at the time, and went on a listening tour—not just across the Walton College, but all across campus. I met with all the deans, as well as with vice provosts, vice chancellors, program directors, and many other leaders. And I listened.

In May 2015, in fact, I scheduled more than seventy meetings that each lasted at least twenty minutes. Before each meeting, I looked up the person I was meeting with using LinkedIn and Google. I almost always found some common bond or connection that I could bring up during our conversation. Ahead of each meeting, I tried to get to know the administrative assistants.

My aim was to get to know other leaders and determine how I could help them. *Was there anything the Walton College was doing that was impeding their progress? Were there ways we could help them succeed?*

I discovered lots of opportunities and got to know many dedicated and professional individuals during that tour. It made a huge difference for me, especially the first year. I learned who to go to when seeking help or feedback. I learned what needed to be done to improve the relationship with other units. And although it wasn't my purpose, I also learned a lot about the operations of the University of Arkansas and the people who were leading the institution. I enjoyed it so much and gained so many benefits that I'm thinking about doing it again.

This sort of activity might feel time consuming, but I'm convinced it actually saves you time in the long run. I was meeting with people who made decisions that affected the Walton College. They were gatekeepers in various processes that I must follow to get things done. Once the relationships were established, the gatekeepers could just call me to get clarification when they had questions or to guide me on modifications I needed to make.

When our chancellor, Joseph Steinmetz, appeared as a guest on one of my podcasts in 2019, we talked about the value of "listening tours." He told me he began the practice because of a mistake he made as dean of the college of arts and sciences at the University of Kansas. When he left Indiana University, he said, he assumed that because the two institutions were similar in so many ways structurally, they also would be similar in their cultures. He was wrong. As a result, he got off to a slow start. He then used a listening tour to correct his course.

"When I went into Kansas," he told me, "one of the first mistakes I made was having that assumption, because I didn't have the information . . . I tried to do some things without the knowledge of what the real culture was at the institution" (Leadership WWeb 2019).

He realized he needed to get to know his new colleagues at a deeper level, so he met with more than fifty leaders throughout the college. And when he became the University of Arkansas chancellor in 2016, Steinmetz made it a point to apply the lesson he'd learned years earlier. During his first six months, he met with seventy-five leaders around campus.

"The real purpose of going around . . . was to understand what that culture actually was more than it was to learn anything about the units," he said. "There was no way I was going to retain the amount of information that I was getting by meeting with all of these groups. But I did get a sense very quickly of what the university valued during those first six months from those meetings" (Leadership WWeb 2019).

Chancellor Steinmetz also embarked on what's become an annual bus tour of the state. The first year, he used the tour mainly for his education. He was new to Arkansas and wanted to learn about its history and its people. In subsequent years, he and his executive committee have used the tour to build relationships and to make presentations on ways the UA can partner with and help solve problems for people in the different regions of Arkansas.

Ongoing, scheduled events to informally listen to the needs of constituents is a huge part of a leader's role. Chancellor Steinmetz meets regularly with student government leaders, and has coffee and donuts once a month with undergraduates, as well as luncheons with faculty members.

As dean, I continue to listen because I am convinced that listening is more important than talking for a leader. But listening doesn't have to be limited to formal interactions. When I park my car and walk to the Business Administration Building, for instance, I start a conversation with a random student along the way.

Hi, I'm Matt. Are you a business major? Have you done an internship? Are you involved in extracurricular activities in the Walton College? Are you involved in any Registered Student Organizations? What do you hope to do when you graduate?

I ask these questions as a part of a normal conversation, being careful not to force it too much. I smile. I make eye contact. And at the end of the conversation, I give them my card with my cell number and tell them to call me if they ever have ideas about how the Walton College can be more EPIC. When I have time, I do the same thing as I walk down the halls or walk to other parts of campus. When students have complaints, I invite them to my office to discuss the issue, or, if I don't have enough time, encourage an associate dean to meet with them. And when I discuss any complaints, I do my best to refrain from defensiveness.

I take a similar approach with faculty. We have lots of formal options for communication, but I want them to know I'm approachable—and that I will approach them. For instance, I often ask our stakeholders, "What would make you prouder of Walton College?"

In 2019, one theme I kept hearing from faculty centered on having an integrity initiative. Only a small percentage of students were taking classes that involved business ethics or integrity, and the faculty recognized the need to increase that emphasis. I agreed, and we ended up hiring Cindy Moehring, who had recently retired as senior vice president and global chief ethics officer for Walmart, to launch our Business Integrity Leadership Initiative—all as a result of listening.

Again, some might think that all of this is too time consuming, but the key is doing it "as you go." It can be tiring, but I try to remember that listening can be the key to competitive advantage. This is an easy step I can take that I'm fairly confident few other business college deans are taking. When

I think like that, my competitive nature drives me forward. Of course, I can't talk individually with all 6,500 students, but I can talk with as many as possible.

Feedback is like gold.

Practicing Procedural Justice

When leaders listen attentively and empathically, we position ourselves to make procedural justice an effective part of our leadership strategy. Procedural justice is a legal term, but I'm applying it to organizational dynamics. The simplified definition? Get people involved.

In the shared governance model used by many universities (including the University of Arkansas), some decisions are made by the faculty, some by the administrators, and some by both. For example, the administration, not the faculty, decides where a new faculty position is allocated, while the faculty makes curriculum decisions. But procedural justice is a process that opens the doors of communication to everyone who has a stake in a decision, regardless of who actually makes the decision.

Shared governance is an excellent method for incorporating procedural justice. It is easy enough for an administrator to see shared governance as an impediment, but it should be viewed as a way to incorporate procedural justice. It helps leaders gain alignment within the organization and get things done quickly and effectively. If you don't have alignment, you may never make progress.

Research has shown that if you allow people to have their say in a matter, they are significantly more likely to feel the decision was fair and will feel more satisfied with the decision that's made (McFarlin and Sweeny 1992). It's a strange thing, but I've seen it play out time and again. This holds up even if people know what they say won't affect the final decision, but it's an even more powerful tool when people know their opinions have weight. On the other hand, if you make decisions without making procedural justice part of the process, those who disagree with the decision often will complain about the process and resist any change that's required. Rather than creating lions who vigorously champion a decision, you empower cultural vipers who poison your efforts.

Tim Scudder, in a chapter he wrote in *The Leaders We Need*, put it this way: "If you are able to accurately reflect their concerns, they'll be more likely to collaborate with you, and if you decide not to do what they ask or suggest, they'll be more likely to understand and accept your decision" (Maccoby and Scudder 2018).

My communication strategy for leadership always includes the best practices of procedural justice. For instance, a key decision I make concerns hiring assistant deans, associate deans, and department heads. When an opening occurs, I review as much information as possible and listen to the opinions of people who will be affected by the outcome, but I make the ultimate hiring decision.[7]

Not long ago, we had an opening for the marketing department chair. After we had narrowed the candidates to two and interviewed both of them, I had a one-hour meeting with the department faculty. I reiterated the process and where we were in that process (management) then spent the next thirty minutes just listening and relating. Even when one faculty member pressed me to discuss my vision for the department, I held firm. I promised to share my thoughts, but not until I had heard from the faculty. I took notes, repeated what I was hearing, and made it crystal clear I was listening to their concerns.

Then, finally, I went through the process again, this time tapping into the sensemaking capability. I said, "Here's where we are today . . . Here's what's going on in the environment . . . This is why we need a certain type of leader with these characteristics." I never said who I planned to hire, but I started discussing the vision for the department. I asked for their input then invented how it was going to happen. I told them the new department chair would have a list of specific objectives in his contract, which is something we typically don't do for department chairs, and that I would review those objectives with him every year. "Here are the ones I've come up with," I said. "What else should I include in there?" That way, they too were involved in the visioning and inventing stages.

At the meeting's end, I said, "You know, I've been here for twenty-four years. When I started in this department as a visiting assistant professor in 1994, every one of you helped me." I started relating to them, including the curmudgeons. We left feeling like we were on the same team because, in fact, we were and are on the same team. We all want the same thing: for the department to be the best it can be.

---

7. In some colleges, faculty vote on the department chair. This practice varies between universities and even between colleges within universities.

At times, I use procedural justice practices because I'm not sure how to solve a particular challenge and I need the collective wisdom (and buy-in) of the college or unit. For instance, in 2019 we held a "Respectful Engagement Town Hall" meeting to discuss the challenges of creating a policy for guest speakers. I asked for this meeting because I had heard of a few instances where guest speakers had made rude and unnecessary comments.

As a public research university, we want to consider uncomfortable perspectives. We want to permit and even encourage speakers who are at times irreverent, nonconforming, or iconoclastic, so long as what they are saying is relevant to the topic. That will stimulate the critical thinking of our students. At the same time, we want to discourage irrelevant comments that are abusive, crude, obscene, vulgar, or inconsiderate.

Those situations don't happen very often, but I wanted to minimize their frequency. It occurred to me that it would be helpful for faculty to have a statement about expectations that they could send to speakers in advance of their guest appearances. I discussed this with several people, including the associate deans. The idea grew to include a statement about collegiality that also would be targeted for faculty, staff, and students, not just guest speakers. This seemed reasonable given that collegiality is one of our four EPIC values.

The faculty have already defined our value of collegiality in the following way: We respect each individual, we value our differences, and we welcome all. And from that we created guidelines for respectful engagement in difficult meetings among colleagues, in interactions between students, and in the classroom—what we called our Respectful Engagement Statement (RES).

The town hall meeting allowed us to hear opinions on what, if anything, we could do to further ensure that we (and our guest speakers) live out this value. Was the current definition of collegiality enough? Did we need something more specific for a complete RES? Did we need something that covered examples of interactions that were not consistent with our RES? Should we create a statement for all audiences or one specific to guest speakers?

There are times, of course, when I forget to involve others in decisions, especially when I'm unusually busy or under a tight deadline. It's not that I don't involve anyone, but I might not involve everyone who should be included. If you become aware that this has happened, it's a good idea to immediately get those people involved. If it is too late for that, you still should acknowledge it to those people and get their perspective. This happened to me more often early in my career than it happens now, because now I realize that I usually make better decisions and get more buy-in from the organization when I incorporate procedural justice.

Opening the Fire Hose

While listening is vital to communication, and, therefore, to leading, every leader also must be heard. What we say and how we say it puts our leadership into motion. If we listen to everyone but then say or do nothing, then we aren't leading. We aren't setting direction, gaining alignment, or inspiring others. We aren't helping people understand their situations or creating inventive solutions to their challenges. As leaders, we have to take what we learn from listening and put it to good use in our actions to truly serve others.

As dean, I have a wide variety of audiences for my communications—our students, potential students, faculty and staff, administration, alumni, the business community, politicians, donors, potential donors, partners, and potential partners. Many of those audiences overlap, and some form special subgroups, like with my advisory committees. I also use a variety of ways to communicate with them—one-on-one interactions, group meetings, town halls, lectures, special events, blogs, articles, podcasts, videos, and social media posts.

When I stepped into the role of dean, I heard from our faculty and staff that they felt as if they hadn't been getting enough information from the dean's office. They wanted greater transparency. I immediately made an effort to change that perception by over-communicating.

Previously, the executive committee of the college would meet once a month and the dean would send an email to the faculty and staff once a semester, sometimes once a year. I went from that to weekly executive committee meetings, weekly emails from the dean, and weekly emails from the associate deans.

The college, in fact, got some sort of communication from the dean's office every day of the workweek. On Monday, it was my "Message from Matt." On Tuesday, it was the minutes from our executive committee meetings. The associate deans took it from there—"Announcements from Anne

(O'Leary-Kelly)" on Wednesday, "Anecdotes from Alan (Ellstrand)" on Wednesday, and "Briefings from Brent (Williams)" on Friday.

I became totally transparent about what was happening in the dean's office. If you look like you're hiding things, you make it easier for rumors and false narratives to take hold in the culture and you effectively create barriers to collaboration. Transparency promotes accountability, trust, and alignment.

My first communication on finances was an exercise in this type of transparency. It ended up taking four weeks, and each email was several pages. I explained in detail to the whole college how much money we had, where it came from, and how it was budgeted. To this day, some other deans at the university read those emails to understand how we operate financially. (And I'll share more on this later in the book.)

There were at least two big benefits of all of this over-communication to my leadership team. One, it forced us to reflect on the details of what we were doing, when we needed to share information, and why and how we should share it. This was particularly helpful to me. As journalist and novelist Joan Didion once put it, "I don't know what I think until I write it down." Similarly, Sir Francis Bacon has said, "Reading maketh a full man; conference a ready man; and writing an exact man." So, writing down and sharing my thoughts caused me and my leadership team to think more carefully and precisely, which made us better leaders. And, two, overcommunicating meant everyone on the leadership team knew what everyone else was doing. There were no surprises, so we worked better as a team.

The faculty and staff also benefited because they were well-informed in a way that fit their primary learning style. It's always important to meet with people in person and to communicate verbally, but academics greatly appreciate the written word. They tend to be oriented toward writing and reading, so communicating in writing gives them the opportunity to truly process the message and think through what it means to them and the people they serve.

On the other hand, daily emails from the dean's office, some of them several pages in length, can eventually become too much of a good thing. It didn't take long before the faculty and staff began to complain about the firehose of information. So, after a couple of years, in 2018 we dialed it back. We still send out the minutes of our executive committee meetings every week. But I now send a faculty and staff email once every two or three weeks, while my associate deans send one about once a month or less.

I communicate regularly with my executive team, including the occasional email over the weekend. But I tell them, in person and in an email at least once a year, that I don't expect them to read or respond to emails I send on Saturdays or Sundays. I like to write emails when they are fresh in my mind and I try to keep them in my outbox over the weekend and send them on Monday. But because I sometimes forget, I want to double-down on clearly communicating my expectations about those emails while emphasizing the importance of relaxing and enjoying time away from work.

I save all of my emails, by the way, and they've become a resource in their own right. I revisit them frequently and several of them are annually updated and sent again. They also provide a treasure trove of examples for how I've used my leadership framework as dean, which is why you'll see them used as examples throughout this book.

The Strategy of Communication

Communication in and of itself is one of the most important leadership strategies a dean can marshal. Entire books, of course, have been written on how to communicate effectively, but what I'm talking about here is using communication strategically. When we communicate effectively, the message we send is received and understood. That's important. When we communicate strategically, our message serves a well-defined purpose that supports the things we hope to achieve. So leaders need to communicate both strategically and effectively.

I began giving this extra attention after I became dean because, frankly, it kept coming up in our meetings, first in our executive committee meetings and later in a faculty and staff meeting. We assigned a task force to help answer the question, *How do we communicate better with the college?* I brought up the question with the deans of other business schools so I could benchmark against their approaches.

One of the things that became apparent was the need to understand the strategic purpose of each of our communications efforts. We have eight methods for communicating with the college, or what we call our *integrating mechanisms*. (1) College-wide emails from the dean's office,

(2) executive committee minutes (shared weekly when we have the meetings), (3) town hall meetings, (4) faculty/staff meetings (two or three per year), (5) breakfast/lunch with the deans, (6) executive committee meetings, (7) college standing committees, and (8) task forces. We have others, including informal integrating mechanisms, but those are the main eight.

The question, then, was what is the primary purpose for each of those mechanisms? When I first started asking that question, either no one knew the answer or different people had different answers. So, we brought clarity to the confusion by assigning each mechanism a purpose: (a) explanation, (b) engagement, and (c) decisions/recommendations (table 7.1).

Here are some guidelines we developed around what we meant by explanation and engagement.

Explanation

- What is going on in the college?
- Why are we engaged in various initiatives or endeavors?
- Who is doing what?
- Why are various decisions being made?
- When will we have meetings or events?
- How are we trying to accomplish our mission and vision?
- Where we are focusing and why?

Engagement

- Involving faculty and staff in the decision-making process by including their feedback, input, and points of view.
- Building collective wisdom and knowledge through discussion and debate.
- Allowing for faculty/staff dialogue on important topics and decisions.

Assigning each mechanism a purpose turned out to be a big deal. We added structure to what was unstructured. People would say, *We go to faculty staff meetings and never make any decisions.* So, we said, *We're not going to make decisions in faculty staff meetings. That's not the purpose. Here's how we're going to make decisions, here's how we're going to engage in dialogue, and here's how we're going to explain things.* Now people know. When they walk into a meeting, they're not thinking they're going to resolve an issue unless that's the stated purpose of the meeting.

Formal Integrating Mechanism	Focus of the Integrating Mechanism			
	Explanation	Engagement	Decisions/ Recommendations	Feedback from College
College-wide emails from the deans	Primary			Secondary
Executive Committee minutes	Primary	Secondary		
Town hall meetings		Primary		Secondary
Faculty and staff meetings	Primary	Secondary	(voting, periodically)	
Informal meeting with deans		Primary		Secondary
Executive Committee meetings		Secondary	Primary	
College standing committees		Primary	Secondary	
College-wide surveys		Secondary		Primary
Task forces		Secondary	Primary	

Table 7.1. WCOB Communications Strategy

The mechanisms we use are part of our strategy for communicating with the college, but I also work hard to think strategically about what and how I communicate. Sometimes I am direct. *Here's the information you need to know. Here's the task you need to do. Here's the question you need to answer.* Other times, my style is subtle, and the message might not be obvious to everyone. But I always try to have a purpose behind everything I say or write.

I learned this strategy, in part, from our chancellor. I remember meetings when he would communicate things that everyone in the room already should have known. Over time, however, I realized he always had a reason. Maybe he was letting us know that he knew something. Or maybe he was using the forum to speak to audiences who weren't even in the room but would read or hear about it later.

One of the ways I've practiced this myself is in our executive committee meetings. The executive committee consists of me, the associate deans, assistant deans, and department chairs—about fifteen people. Students, members of other committees, and guests often join us to present information we need to know. We typically meet once a week during the fall and spring semesters, and we send out the meeting minutes the next day. The committee makes decisions and recommendations that affect everyone in the college, so reading the minutes has become ingrained in our culture. You'll be hard pressed to find anyone in the college who doesn't at least skim over the minutes, and many faculty and staff members read them very closely.

The minutes, of course, provide information about the decisions and recommendations, as well as about the process that went into making those decisions. When the minutes go out, I often make sure that words like *voted on*, *decided*, or *passed* are in bold font so they are easily recognized. The minutes also provide an opportunity for me, as dean, to communicate more indirectly on certain topics.

For instance, consider the following scenario. I learn about a false rumor circulating through the college, so I send out an email explaining it's not true. That sounds sensible, but it might not be the best way to go. In many cases, it's more effective if I say what is true during an executive committee meeting. The truth becomes part of the minutes, everyone reads the minutes, so everyone now knows the truth. I have addressed the rumor without coming across as defensive and without calling anyone out about spreading it. I haven't even acknowledged the rumor.

I also use the minutes to reinforce key messages. When I ask the executive committee to brainstorm ways we can better support our priority for research and then implement some of their ideas, it sends a message (through the minutes) that we're not just paying lip service to the importance of research. Or I might include agenda items about policies and procedures as a reminder to the college that we take those things seriously. For instance, I might open a meeting with a reminder that if faculty members join a board, even if it's something they do in their free time, they need to complete a non-conflict of interest form.

Here's an entry in the minutes of April 2, 2018, that illustrates how I spoke to the entire college about Title IX compliance simply by mentioning it in our executive committee meeting: "Matt reminded the committee that with regard to sexual misconduct, harassment and assault, if you hear or see something, you must say something. It is everyone's responsibility in the college. Any allegations must be reported to Title IX coordinator Tyler Farrar."

To use the minutes of a meeting as a communication strategy, by the way, you need a really smart executive assistant who takes good notes and writes well when summarizing the meeting. I'm fortunate to have that in Lori Foster, who makes almost every aspect of my job easier.

Using meeting minutes is just one way to communicate strategically. The bigger point is to use your words purposefully. You may have to say things several times, using multiple mechanisms, to get a point across, so always think through who will hear or read a message, what they will do with it, why it will matter to them, and how you'd like them to respond. And never take communication for granted.

Communication in Crisis

The COVID-19 pandemic that began in 2020 presented a number of challenges for leaders at all levels all across the world, but in some ways the crisis helped us grow our communication skills at the Walton College. We were forced out of our comfort zones, and that compelled us to innovate, adapt howing we communicated with each other at a time when clear, informative messaging was critical.

Like every other university, we moved all of our classes to remote during the middle of the Spring 2020 semester, requiring some faculty who had never taught remotely or online[8] to quickly learn new educational technologies so they could deliver their content. Our Executive MBA program already had a blended delivery,[9] so the faculty who had

---

8. Remote means that everyone in the class meets at the same time (synchronous); online means that most of the content is asynchronous and that the course was specifically designed for an online environment. A course where some students meet in person in the classroom while some are remote is referred to as hybrid.

9. For the Executive MBA program, students come in once per month for a face-to-face meeting. The rest of the content is online. Students are from different states, and so they are familiar with collaborating remotely.

taught in that program had no trouble making the transition. We also already had three fully online undergraduate degree programs: general business, accounting, and supply chain management. So our faculty who had taught in those programs were in good shape. Plus, most of our faculty use our learning management system even if they don't teach online, and that system has online capabilities. Still, there was a learning curve for some, and lots of communication was required, even for those who were experts at online teaching.

We had to make quick decisions about policies and procedures related to all aspects of college life, from how we taught classes, to how we planned, to how we managed access to our facilities. Some decisions were made by others, but most were collaboration, all while practicing a new term that entered our lexicon—social distancing. And everyone—students, parents, faculty, staff, alumni, and other external partners—had legitimate questions that we needed to answer.

We didn't have much time to make the transition. Fortunately, our spring break occurred the week following the announcement that we were going online, so faculty could use that time to get adjusted. A great deal of communication was needed and lots of questions had to be answered. Some faculty wanted to come to their offices to make videos of their lectures with the classroom tools they were familiar with. There were questions about learning assessments that would not be possible online. There were questions about how to prevent cheating with online testing. There were questions about when we would be back in the classroom.

It soon became clear that we were not going to return to the classroom that semester and that we'd have to postpone commencement until after June 1. This wasn't going to be a temporary fix where we were teaching remotely for a few weeks and then everything would return to normal.

Our leadership team sent emails to faculty and staff explaining that perfection was not the goal in this crisis. Some of our students had lost their jobs, some of their parents were losing their businesses and jobs, and some of their relatives were getting COVID-19. We all—faculty, staff, and administrators—needed to be extremely accommodating and caring.

At the same time that we were communicating information to the faculty and staff, we needed to be cognizant of their emotions and uncertainty. And we needed them to communicate with their students about the unique plans for their specific course. I'm proud to say our faculty and staff made this transition with excellence, professionalism, innovation, and collegiality.

One of the things we learned during the experience was how to make better use of technology to communicate with each other. Because we had to leave campus and work from home, we all started using Microsoft Teams. I had never used this component of Microsoft Office, but one of our faculty members had been advocating for it even before the pandemic. On what turned out to be my last day in the office before I began working from home, I began exploring its features and subsequently started using it every day.

Using Microsoft Teams, we set up several teams of our own: The Walton College COVID Pandemic Team, the Walton College Dean Team, the Executive Committee team, a team with the deans of other colleges and the provost, and many other university-wide teams. At first I was using Microsoft Teams mainly for video meetings, but each day I discovered new capabilities, including task assignment, collaboration tools, document sharing tools, and more. It is really a workflow management solution that improved my effectiveness as a manager and leader.

At one point, the Dean Team—Anne, Alan, Brent and I—decided to make a video using Microsoft Teams because it allows you to record your meetings, save them as mp4 files, host them on YouTube, and then distribute them. So we began distributing weekly videos of ourselves to the faculty and staff of the college. Because each of us was working from home, the videos had an informal feel as we talked to each other and shared information and encouragement with faculty and staff.

I also realized I could use the video feature for some of my marketing projects. For instance, I had recorded about eighty episodes of our Be Epic podcast, but all of them had been recorded in person. We had published sixty-three of the episodes when we began working remotely, so we still had about three months of safety stock. But I realized that I could use Teams to record new interviews remotely, if needed.

I prefer recording podcasts in person, just as I prefer meeting with people face to face. The pandemic changed that aspect of my communication in many ways that technology couldn't easily replicate. We had to cancel several banquets, awards ceremonies, executive education programs, and my board meetings.

I felt so bad for the students who were missing all of these events, and even worse for the graduating seniors and graduating graduate school students who might miss out on graduation. I love commencement because it is a celebration of student academic achievement.

Like our faculty and staff, however, our students proved adaptable, patient, and selfless throughout what proved to be a difficult period in our global history. And ultimately I'm convinced that this crisis made all of us more effective students, teachers, researchers, and administrators.

CHAPTER 8

Socializing Our Narrative

I f the dean is the only one who believes in and communicates the mandate of the college, then he or she is the only one who will even attempt to carry it out. But if you socialize the narrative—allow others to help create it and share it—then the message will take root in your culture.

For me, this approach began serendipitously with an off-site strategy meeting of my executive committee shortly after I was named interim dean in 2015. At the time, the Walton College was going through the accreditation process with the Association to Advance Collegiate Schools of Business (AACSB), so the stated objective for the meeting that summer was for us to make the business case for moving the college to a level more on par with other top schools. We studied things like our enrollment trends, our faculty size, our faculty quality, the pay of our faculty and staff, and the resources of our PhD programs. We identified the gaps between "us and them" in terms of programs, people, and facilities (but not money) and built a business case for attaining the resources (including money) to close those gaps.

We held a five-hour session in the conference room of Field Agent, an entrepreneurial tech company a few miles from campus. We brought in lunch and went to work. The atmosphere was focused but relaxed—people wore shorts or jeans, and sports coats weren't allowed—and the group was incredibly productive.

My role, to link this back to my leadership framework, was to set direction, align the team to a shared vision, and motivate and inspire. One of the ways I did that all of those things was by communicating the goals before we met and telling everyone what they needed to do to prepare. But I also entered that initial meeting with the mandate fully memorized. Plus, I had memorized historical dates about when the college was formed, when we were first accredited, and other key milestones and facts and figures that were relevant to our discussions. That preparation made it incredibly easy to provide sensemaking, to relate to the people and their ideas, to provide a compelling vision, and to be inventive when the discussions slowed.

Late in the day, we addressed a question about how we could persuade stakeholders to provide the support we needed to close the gaps we had identified. And that question, along with the discussions leading up to it, resulted in the most important output of the day: "The Epic of Walton College."

The initial version, referred to back then as "the story," was about 1,200 words of narrative that used the story of the college to make a case for the resources we needed to compete at the highest level. It began in 1998 with the $50 million donation from the Walton Family Charitable Support Foundation because that gift provided the initial impetus for separating us from most state university business schools. It funded research, helped us attract top faculty, and allowed us to expand or create outreach centers like the Center for Retail Excellence. We also created a Global Engagement Office, developed a Walton College Honors Program, increased scholarships and fellowships, and established a state-of-the-art behavioral business research laboratory. Our departments and programs shot up the rankings. We began attracting top students not only from within Arkansas, but from around the world.

This was a great story to tell because we could paint a portrait of how the Walton College had lived out its mandate in the past and how we were living it in the present, while also providing our vision for taking it into the future. The story empirically showed not only our growth but the positive impact of that growth on the college, the university, and the state. It also showed what we needed to move forward. The initial gift was an endowment, and market fluctuations had limited its growth to about 1.17 percent a year. This was straining our ability to keep pace with the growth that the gift itself had made possible. We knew the path and we knew the target, but we needed more resources to get there. The story helped make that case.

From the original narrative, we created a slide presentation to use when we shared the story during meetings with stakeholders. There were thirty-two slides in the deck, but it was highly customizable based on the executive team member who was presenting and who was in the audience. The slides were light on words and heavy on visuals, but the notes sections were rich in content so the presenter could share personal examples and illustrations while easily accessing the foundational content.

The next year, we put the story through an in-depth editing process to clarify our identity as a college to a wider variety of constituents. In other words, we developed versions that would speak more clearly to prospective students, parents, alumni, and other stakeholders. This was the idea of my senior associate dean, Anne O'Leary-Kelly, who is very creative and studies identity theory as a key part of her research in management.

In 2017, we looked at the narrative again, this time in light of how well our strategic plan aligned with our mission and values. Then we modified our strategy based on what we learned.

We now call the story "The Epic of Walton College," which gives it an obvious double-meaning because it refers to our EPIC values and to the traditional definition of *epic* as a work portraying a journey with heroic deeds in a grand adventure. It is revised and updated every year. In 2019, we expanded it considerably.

For starters, we added a great deal more about our history. While the Walton donation was an extraordinary booster shot in our journey, it wasn't the beginning. The Walton College traces its roots to 1926, and we wanted the narrative to honor the former faculty, staff, students, and donors who helped make it worthy of the Walton Family Foundation's donation. We also included details about the accomplishments of the college, the vision for the future, and how we can achieve that future.

In the past, the executive committee was responsible for updating the narrative, and each member was encouraged to involve others from within their departments or units. In 2019, however, we took that a step further and, as part of my commitment to procedural justice, sought input from several individuals in units that I felt were not well represented in the story. All of them were enthusiastic, helpful, and grateful for being included, but one in particular became an unusually big champion of the narrative. Finally, I solicited feedback on input from the entire college.

As we sought additional input, I made it clear that we could not include every story or have an exhaustive history of the college. We wanted it to be a relatively short read, and keeping it tight was, and is, challenging. As I go about my work, I'm continually finding stories, facts, and ideas that I think might fit into the narrative. If they don't make the cut, they wind up being used for other purposes.

At this point you might be thinking that the greatest value of creating the story of your college is that it will help you make presentations to potential donors. That's important, but we use the narrative in a variety of ways.

- It's a good place to start when we create videos about the strategic direction of the college because it provides a framework, possible first draft text, and supporting facts and figures.
- We use it to answer questions from donors or others who might be interested in our stewardship. Donors sometimes want reports on how their endowments are being used. Various parts of the narrative can be lifted and used to provide the context for a stewardship report. It is easy for a leadership team to assume donors know more than they actually know, so various parts of the narrative can provide context. Major donors who provide sizable endowments need to understand how their gifts fit into the overall story.
- We use it to identify long-term trends in the college and strategic opportunities. Reading the narrative carefully and reflecting on it can help the leadership team see logical strategic progressions that would be hard to see otherwise. In this regard, it is a tool for helping the leadership team with sensemaking, a key leadership capability.
- It helps us identify vestigial processes, policies, or organizational structures. Such elements may no longer be needed, but thinking through the history of the organization can help you understand how they originated and also help you develop the logic as to why they need to change.
- It can help future leadership teams understand the context of where the college is today and why we are going in the direction that we are going. A new leadership team may or may not agree with the direction, but at least they will understand the rationale behind it. In areas where they don't agree with the direction, it will help them craft the rationale to change. And in areas where they agree, it gives them a good foundation to build upon the strategic direction. When faculty who have been around for a long time become aware that the new leadership team understands the narrative of the college, they may be more accepting of changes in direction. When new leadership teams come in, there are always people longing to explain the college's historical context. The narrative can help to

relieve some of this pressure, which is good for the faculty, staff, and the new leadership team.

There's one more way we get value from the narrative, and it's related to the culture of the college.

The executive committee took ownership of the story, because they wrote it and refined it. All of a sudden, my leadership team agreed on where we came from, where we were, and where we were going. On top of that, when we did the edits, they came up with facts and figures I didn't know about and added those to the narrative. They greatly improved the quality of the information, which greatly improved the quality of any presentation I made, whether it was to our MBA advisory committee, a civic group, or the board of a charitable trust.

By sharing the epic with the rest of the college, our faculty and staff also take greater ownership of their part in our story. This is particularly true for new members of our team, as I learned in an email from Donnie Williams, who became executive director of our Supply Chain Research Center in 2019.

"Thank you for sharing this," he wrote after I sent the narrative out for feedback in Fall 2019. "This really helps me, as a new faculty member, to understand the history and roots of the Walton College. This also helps me understand more clearly my role and how what I work on each day supports the overall mission of the college. These are truly exciting times to be at the Walton College and I am blessed to be here."

Creating, maintaining, and socializing this narrative has contributed immensely to the health of our culture. That has made sharing the story something more heartfelt and genuine than any fabricated sales pitch.

CHAPTER 9

Marketing Our Narrative

While "The Epic of Walton College" was becoming well-known within the college and well-used in presentations, our successes weren't effectively being shared to broader audiences until after I had an eye-opening experience that changed my thinking and our approach to marketing the narrative.

In April 2017, I spent the first half hour of a biannual Dean's Executive Advisory Board meeting reporting on the most recent accomplishments of the Walton College. Frankly, I was feeling really good about it. I figured the update would generate a nice round of applause and a few words of praise that would launch us into the rest of the meeting with some positive vibes.

When I finished, one of the board members stood up.

"Dean Waller, this is great," he said. "Clearly, the Walton College has prospered in many ways over the past six months. In fact, the college has seen significant improvements over the past few years."

I was feeling even better about the presentation.

Then the other shoe dropped, metaphorically speaking, and it ricocheted up and hit me right between the eyes.

"Why is it that no one knows about these improvements?" the board member said. "You all teach marketing, but you clearly don't practice it."

Other board members were nodding their heads in agreement, and some began piling on. Later, several board members talked about it with me privately. Some sent me examples of marketing literature they were receiving from other business schools, advertisements from business newspapers and magazines, and links to impressive websites of other business schools.

I'll never forget that meeting. It was painful, but it was exactly what I needed. Every dean should covet that type of tough love from an advisory board because such truth provides the impetus for positive change. Excellence is one of our values at the Walton College, and we don't need to pridefully stick our heads in the sand when we're falling short of living it out. We need to own it and fix it.

As the dean, I took the criticism personally because it exposed an area where my leadership was falling short. I knew the Walton College was endowed with marketing expertise, both on our faculty and on our staff. I also knew some of the most innovative marketing companies in the world were located within a few miles of our campus and were led by our alumni. There was no reason we couldn't excel in marketing the Walton College.

Furthermore, we had every reason imaginable to make the effort and investment needed to excel. A strong approach to marketing would help us implement our vision of using teaching, research, and service to be thought leaders and catalysts for transforming lives.

Our thought leadership springs from our teaching, research, and service. Great marketing around our thought leadership would add value to students, faculty, and the business community—not just at and around the University of Arkansas, but at universities and in communities all over the world. And by adding that value, we would become more effective catalysts for transforming lives.

What we lacked was a commitment to a well-conceived philosophy and strategy for putting cutting-edge marketing into practice. We lacked direction, alignment, and motivation. We lacked leadership.

I took responsibility for this leadership shortfall and vowed to do something about it. So in addition to my regular work during the summer of 2017, I spent time and energy researching strategies and tactics for marketing the Walton College. I spent hours talking about it with my associate deans, students, faculty, staff, alumni, board members, and consultants. I read books and blogs, and I listened to podcasts. In sum, I sought input from every source I could. It became clear that marketing was essential to implementing our vision, but only if we elevated our approach. And that's exactly what we've tried to do.

A Word on Marketing

Bob Casey, the former curator of transportation at The Henry Ford, once pointed out the difference between an invention and an innovation.

"An invention is something that is new and interesting," he said. "An innovation is something new and interesting that gets widely adopted. If you can't get it widely adopted, it may be cool, but it's not an innovation because it's not really affecting the lives of very many people."[10]

Innovation has a lasting impact, and marketing is one way we can ensure our best practices, innovative ideas, and success stories make a transformative difference in people's lives.

The American Marketing Association defines marketing as "the activity, set of institutions, and processes for creating, communicating, delivering, and exchanging offerings that have value for customers, clients, partners, and society at large" (AMA 2021).

While every word in that definition matters, for me it hinges on one in particular: *value*. In fact, our approach to marketing the Walton College of Business hinges on two forms of that one word: *value* and *values*. We believe marketing is about providing value while honoring our values. Value is what we provide in our marketing offerings. Values are what we honor with our marketing offerings.

We add value by producing marketing that solves problems for our constituents. For instance, thought leadership is at work throughout the college in our teaching, research, and service, but its value falls short without marketing. Having a potentially innovative pedagogical method, for example, may be great content for thought leadership, but it is insufficient if no other faculty members learn about it and implement it in their research or courses. True thought leadership happens when other faculty get onboard with the new and effective method. Achieving that requires marketing.

Similarly, faculty members may advance a theory in their field in a very significant way and even publish it in a top journal. True thought leadership, in this case, occurs if other researchers use this advancement in their research and if practitioners improve in their discipline by using the ideas. Spreading the word to those audiences requires marketing.

Thought leadership isn't the only way we add value. In fact, the concept of adding value hit home for me when I discovered the third-most visited page on our webpage was a blog titled, "Six Steps to Hiring Interns." If you had googled "hiring interns," it was the second link to come up. In addition, seven other completely unrelated websites linked to this blog. The page was giving us tremendous visibility, and most of the leaders in the Walton

---

10. https://www.thehenryford.org/explore/stories-of-innovation/what-if/henry-ford/

College didn't even know the blog existed. The article was wordy and the page design was not very impressive, but recruiters from all over were reading it. Why? It provided information that helped them do their jobs.

Marketing provides value, and it's values-driven. We honor our values by producing offerings that live up to our stated values—not only our four core values but also the mission and vision they support. Marketing is driven by our mandate. Our mission and vision are part of our brand promise, and we deliver on that promise by providing marketing that adds value. It's how we prove to the world that we really are who we say we are.

Building a Marketing Team

By the end of that summer of 2017, I had reached the conclusion that a fresh approach to our marketing had to provide value and it had to honor our values. It had to solve problems for our constituents, and it had to be EPIC. This became our driving philosophy for marketing the college.

To create the specifics of our plan and to execute it, of course, I needed help. That help came primarily in the form of three groups—the internal marketing team at the Walton College, a newly created Marketing Advisory Board, and a marketing consulting firm.

Our internal marketing team is part of our development and external relations department. Within that unit, the senior director of communications oversees a marketing and communications officer (who oversees the college's social media and advertising), an assistant director of creative services (who makes sure everyone follows the branding guidelines), a graphic designer, and a website manager. Seven other people in that unit focus mostly on development-related work but also at times help with marketing initiatives.

Soon after I became dean, I asked this group to come up with a tagline for the college. My favorite organizational tagline was "Think Different" from Apple. I had seen a grainy seven-minute video of former Apple CEO Steve Jobs announcing that tagline and a corresponding brand campaign, so I shared that story with my team.

It's hard to imagine now, but the video shows Jobs, in 1997, standing on a small stage and talking about how the Apple brand had suffered from neglect and was losing its relevance and vitality. The company was spending a fortune on advertising, he said, but you wouldn't know it, because the messages focused on "speeds and fees" and "bits and mega-hertz" rather than Apple's core value.

Here's how he summed up Apple's core value: "We believe that people with passion can change the world for the better" (Jobs 1997). Then he launched a new brand-marketing campaign by showing a commercial that didn't mention computers or technology. Instead, it celebrated the "crazy ones" who have changed the world and ended with the now-famous tagline: Think Different.

I told our team the Walton College needed a tagline that reflected our values in a similarly clear, simple, and elegant fashion. They responded to the challenge by coming up with a two-word tagline, Be Epic. I loved it right away, and we rolled it out in 2016. Not only did it remind me of "Think Different," but it totally fit our brand and our needs. (1) It included the acronym for our values. (2) It was a call to action tied to our vision of serving as a catalyst for transforming lives. (3) It was simple. (4) It was easy to understand.

Needless to say, I was very proud of that team, and it was a great lesson for me. I didn't realize how much capacity and creativity they had, so their work reminded me that people will rise to the occasion when given the opportunity. Creating the Be Epic tagline helped them to become more epic. Now I lean on them not only for tactical marketing help but also for strategic marketing input.

The second group that's been key to our plan is our Marketing Advisory Board. It consists of eight faculty members who are well-respected teachers or influential researchers, many with significant platforms on LinkedIn or another social media platform. They represent a broad range of academic departments, and most of them are innovative teachers or subject matter experts (SMEs) on various topics.

The third group is Modthink, a consulting firm we hired to help us develop difficult-to-emulate marketing processes. Modthink was founded by Walton MBA alumnus Brent Robinson, and it is located on historic Dickson Street in Fayetteville, Arkansas, less than two miles from my office. Brent got involved in digital marketing in 2007, worked for one of the first social media influencer agencies, and built a strong business with proven results. But I also wanted an agency that was close to campus and that understood our college, and Brent was an active alumnus who, among other things, had served on one of my advisory boards.

Other people and groups got involved as we developed and implemented our plan, but those three were foundational to launching our efforts and remain heavily involved in the execution.

Implementing Our Value(s)

The more we worked on upgrading our approach to marketing, the more I learned about things like ecommerce marketing, digital marketing, inbound marketing, social media marketing, and influencer marketing. Advertising, marketing literature, and our website presence were still important, but I wanted our marketing processes to be based more on new media than old media.

When we began benchmarking our current practices, I also realized that most of the marketing literature, websites, and advertisements used by other business colleges could be emulated with enough money. But it occurred to me that doing so would not lead to a sustainable competitive advantage. If we could create marketing processes that were difficult to replicate, while at the same time creating lots of value for our constituents, then we would have a competitive advantage.

So we knew our marketing needed to provide value and honor our values, we knew it needed to be based more on new media than old media, and we knew we needed to invent processes that were difficult for others to emulate. With all that in mind, we established a long-term goal for what success would look like: "By May 2021, the Walton College will have the most effective thought-leader-driven marketing of any public business school in the United States." Then we began crafting a plan to make it happen.

Frankly, it was a big plan. I knew it would take us several years to implement our vision for a marketing strategy, and we no doubt would pivot several times along the way. But inventing and visioning aren't really happening when leaders set the bar low and essentially only mimic what's already being done. Leaders have to evaluate the risks and make smart decisions, so I'm not talking about chasing every rabbit that hops into your field. But part of leadership is discerning when the opportunity is there to go big, and then not shrinking from the challenge.

I'd like to give you a feel for how this has played out, and continues to play out, for the marketing of the Walton College. To that end, I'm going to share the bigger vision ideas we laid out in our plan, and then give you some examples of what we've already done.

Fully implementing our grand marketing strategy will require that we add some combination of the capabilities of a media company and a software-as-a-Server (SaaS) provider to our model for educating students. In the not-to-distant future, in fact, I envision these two capabilities becoming staples of successful business schools. Not only will they impact how we teach students but also how we market the college.

Even before the coronavirus pandemic forced universities to use online methods, we realized that business schools that only rely on the classroom, simplistic lecture videos, and the syndication of educational content through learning management systems (LMS) would fall behind. Adding the aspects of a media company will allow us to create core capabilities for content creation, including video, audio, and print, as well as an omni-channel syndication of that content.

The content doesn't always need to be high quality; some of it needs to be just-in-time—recorded on a smartphone, for example. Story-telling and gamification will be salient characteristics of the content. In many cases, the educational content will go out using a freemium model where it is given away through many channels, including social media, video, podcasts, and blogs. Premium content will be available along with certifications, micro-credentials, academic credits, and degrees.

The syndication will focus on solving problems for narrow student segments, so we need to create the content in a way that is economical to slice, dice, and repurpose for various constituents—executives, professionals who are attempting to pivot in their roles, professionals who are trying to advance in their careers, as well as students wanting a bachelor's or advanced degree in business. We can't just put the content on multiple channels; rather, it must be optimized by channel and by persona, and it needs to spark discussion among students and practitioners.

We can record a lecture by a faculty member, for example, and then use the content for a number of purposes. The lecture text could be rewritten to create content for multiple blogs and posts in a variety of channels. Or a faculty member might create a slide deck for a course, and parts of it could be repurposed for blogs and social media posts.

We also can take research published in peer-reviewed academic journals (including articles by faculty at other universities), extract the core value-added content, and paraphrase it in a way that credits the author and is widely consumable by business practitioners. And we can do interviews with the coauthors, which can be distributed as both video and audio podcasts.

By repurposing peer-reviewed journal articles and major educational content, we can achieve economies of scope and, therefore, make the offerings efficient enough to be sustainable. It also reduces the total effective cost of research and of creating teaching content.

Business schools also will evolve to provide SaaS, the model where licensed software is delivered to subscribers over the Internet, and that, too, will become a key part of our marketing efforts. Professors in the business school, for instance, often create scales to measure constructs of individuals or firms, and they teach about the scales created by other researchers. Among others, there are scales for leadership based on concepts like visioning, scales on management based on concepts like planning, and scales on organizational effectiveness based on concepts like innovation. Faculty also develop and teach about business tools, including tools for forecasting, pricing, or measuring uncertainty.

All these scales and tools could be made available on the business school's website in the form of a SaaS that would create valuable information for users. In many cases, the software could be offered in a freemium model. Regardless, the software and its results, just like the content we create, has to be high-quality information that truly solves problems for our constituents. If we provide that value in these software offerings, it will grow and strengthen our brand.

At the same time, our marketing efforts can't become a burden on professors, especially those who are active in research. They don't need to focus on repurposing content or creating SaaS offerings, although they are essential sources for the original, pillar content. So we will need to create well-designed, innovative business processes and build technical teams using internal staff, outsourced experts, and consultants.

The technical teams include writers, editors, project managers, graphics designers, social media professionals, audio specialists, videographers, web developers, and others. These teams will help create and implement a process for selecting journal articles, turning them into pillar content, syndicating the pillar content, parsing the pillar content and repurposing it for social media channels, selecting interviewees for podcasts and video interviews, producing those interviews, turning the interviews into blogs, and parsing out the audio, video, and blogs to various social media channels.

Each repurposing, parsing, and syndication must be done with a strategic focus on the student or alumni persona. The offerings will target personas whose psychographics include various combinations of three main factors—how they value security, status, and developing their network. Students in business schools engage with the college based on these three constructs, so we need to define and serve a plethora of narrow student segment personas.

Making Progress

When I think about our marketing efforts in the context of the startup J-curve, I recognize that we have done a great deal of creating and several aspects have been released. Most parts of it already are morphing, which puts us in the bottom of the curve, and in a few areas we've begun to model and scale in an upward trend.

Frankly, I'm excited by how much progress we made in a short amount of time. Here are some of the methods that already have become a part of our approach:

Feedback loops. To solve problems for our constituents, we need to understand their challenges, what we're already doing well, and where we need to improve. For instance, when we realized that the blog on hiring interns was so popular, we dug deeper to find out why. We talked to some recruiters to understand why they were reading the article, what they liked about it, and how we could improve it. Then we brainstormed additional ideas of our own.

We eventually made improvements to the content and readability of the article and the page design, and we added helpful links and buttons that made it easier to learn more or connect with our student interns. Now that article provides greater value to recruiters, as well as to our Career Center and to our students by helping more of them land internships. It also strengthened our brand value. We wanted that webpage to scream excellence, professionalism, innovation and collegiality. We wanted it to be EPIC.

Our marketing strategy now includes a broad performance measurement system along with a continuous improvement system. We're using a variety of tools to monitor and measure what we're doing with marketing, and that allows us to improve our efficiency and the overall effectiveness of our efforts. For instance, our reviews have led us to clean up the college's social media presence so that all of the accounts use the same logos and follow our brand guidelines and the university's brand guidelines. The reviews also led us to create a content calendar to better manage the workflow. The systems themselves are difficult for competitors to emulate, as are many of the improvements that have resulted from those systems. That gives us a competitive marketing advantage.

We also started using the Net Promoter Score in conjunction with other measures to understand if we are treating our constituents well. The NPS was created in 2003 by Fred Reichheld, a partner at Bain & Company. One version of the questions we ask is, "On a scale from 0 to 10, how probable is it that you would recommend the Walton College to a friend who is considering business school?" People who select from zero to six are classified as detractors; people who select seven or eight are considered passives; people who select nine and ten are called promoters. To calculate the NPS, you take the percentage of people who are promoters and subtract the percentage of people who are distractors. We also ask open-ended questions such as, "What are the greatest strengths of the Walton College?" and "What are the areas needing improvement in the Walton College?"

We administer this survey to all undergraduates and MBA students. For the graduating MBA students, we also include an exit interview.

In August 2020, during the pandemic and just before classes started, we sent a survey to all of our students in the Walton College to assess their sentiments. This short questionnaire began with the usual Net Promoter Score question. We followed this with a section on the impacts of COVID-19, a section on the effectiveness of our education during social distancing in face-to-face classes as well as remote teaching, and a final section related to diversity and inclusion. The first-wave survey went out just before classes started and the second wave went out a couple of weeks after classes began. We sent additional waves during the semester, and we're using the results to improve processes, policies, and communication.

In addition to surveys, we began using mystery shoppers to improve our marketing. Mystery shoppers, sometimes called secret shoppers, help an organization test and measure the quality of things like customer service, job performances, regulatory compliance, and messaging. They do the things a typical customer would do, and then create a report on their experience and their results.

Any program that can have a mystery-shopping study in the Walton College will have one, including things like student advising and recruiting processes, but we started by mystery shopping the experiences potential students have when they seek information about our Executive MBA program. Our consulting firm had "shoppers" visit and then evaluate our website and the websites of several of our competitors. They weren't looking at the application process, but things like forms we asked them to fill out, calls to action, the usability of landing pages, thank-you emails, and other follow-up marketing.

Their report provided great insight into what we did well, what other Executive MBA programs did well (and poorly), and where we might improve the ways we present and collect information and follow-up with potential students who show an interest in the program. All of the programs we looked at had room for improvement, but we were looking for the best ideas. We found them and began implementing them.

The surveys and mystery shoppers produced feedback that resulted in a complete makeover of our MBA websites. For instance, these are some improvements we made to the users' experience:

- Low barrier forms that only required a name and email address
- A thank-you page with inspiring imagery
- A thank-you page with direct contact information
- A clear statement in the thank you that someone would be in contact the next working day
- Links to information about the application process in the follow-up email
- A call to action in a follow-up email encouraging the person to apply to the program
- A confirmation email written in first person
- Follow-up emails with links to interesting blogs written by the business school
- Links to the business school's social media accounts in correspondence
- Links to student and alumni success stories
- Follow up email based on optional questions about specific interests

In addition to making it look better visually and function better practically, the team used feedback to identify the specific themes the site should emphasize with its message.

One theme is value—we want to communicate that the Walton MBA and Executive MBA (EMBA) delivers high-quality learning at an affordable cost compared to similar schools. We have a great faculty, great learning experiences, financial support, strong placement outcomes, and students who are successful after they graduate.

The second theme is that the learning is both innovative and fun. The EMBA includes support like tutors for quantitative courses, we have outstanding guest speakers, we have a global immersion component, and we enroll a high-quality and diverse cohort of students. The content about the full-time MBA focuses on the innovative track classes, highlights the internship experience and professional development, and emphasizes that we personalize and customize the program. As far as the fun, the site communicates our commitment to networking and social events, clubs, alumni events, and social responsibility.

The third theme is our unique corporate connections. The companies in our region work with us to enhance our program, offer professional development, host site visits, provide guest speakers, and contribute to our curriculum.

We did a similar remodel of the website for our Master of Science in Economic Analytics, a key program that meets a growing need in our data-rich business world. The upgrades to these sections of our website are just one way marketing plays a key part in the continuous improvement process so that we can innovate based on insights from feedback.

Psychographic Information. One key to any successful marketing strategy is to collect rich psychographic information about constituent groups. Feedback surveys are part of that process, but we want to collect more than just opinions in questionnaires about what we're already doing. To go deeper, we began using interviews and focus groups, starting with my advisory boards and then with groups of other constituents.

With alumni, we might ask questions like *Why did you choose the Walton College to pursue your degree?* Or *What value does your Walton College degree bring to your professional life?* For a group of recruiters, we might ask, *What value do students from the Walton College bring to the companies that hire them?*

Psychographic-oriented data is subjective, and using it together with objective demographic data gives us deep insights into things like why alumni participate on advisory boards or give money to the college. For instance, when we surveyed my Dean's Executive Advisory Board, we learned that 94 percent of the respondents grew up in Arkansas and 77 percent of them participated in the Greek system while in college. Through additional questions and interviews, we learned that they primarily joined the board out of a sense of duty and a desire to help the college reach higher levels of prominence. They value the relationships they build with one another, students, faculty, and staff, and they believe their participation helps them professionally in many ways, including networking, learning new concepts, and credibility. They want to help develop the reputation of the Walton College through financial support, serving as an ambassador, and providing internships and jobs to our students. They want to learn about and interact with our students, and they would like us to become more diverse as a college.

Demographic data tells us things like how philanthropy relates to age, business ownership, and so on. But some retired business owners find fulfillment in helping students succeed, while others are more focused on leaving a legacy with their family name attached to it. The messages we communicate, the philanthropic initiatives we offer, and the focus of the conversation will be very different for these two different psychographic segments.

Similarly, if we know the psychographics of our EMBA market segments, then we can target Facebook ads to professionals who have liked specific pages or identified particular interests. We also can determine which hashtags these market segments use on Twitter and LinkedIn, and then we can focus tweets and LinkedIn posts to those groups.

Blogs. We created a landing page called Walton Insights to house our blogs. And once an article is published on Walton Insights, we often publish a "teaser" as a LinkedIn article, make a LinkedIn post about it, Tweet it, and post it on Facebook. But we don't just write blogs and post them. These blogs must provide value, and our process for producing them is part of our competitive advantage because it's difficult to emulate.

The blogs typically fit into three categories: thought-leadership blogs, helpful blogs, and rah-rah blogs.

The rah-rah blogs usually celebrate someone in or connected to the college, like an alumni or student spotlight. We need rah-rah blogs because part of our strategy is using marketing to achieve our vision and mission. Rah-rah blogs add value by celebrating excellence in role models in a way that inspires, motivates, and rewards people, so they serve as a catalyst for transforming lives.

The helpful blogs provide information someone can use. They add value by addressing specific challenges people face, like the blog on hiring interns or another we titled, "The Complete Guide to Selecting a Business Major." Since a key part of our marketing approach is solving problems for our constituents, this blog was a direct hit.

These blogs are a form of inbound marketing, which is also key to our overall strategy. Outbound marketing, for instance, would use advertisements to spread the message about our online undergraduate program. Inbound marketing involves blogs like, "How to Know If You Should Get Your Business Degree Online," "Picking Your Perfect University for Earning an Online Business Degree," and "The Complete Guide to Selecting a Business Major"—all without necessarily mentioning our specific program. These blogs address real questions people have when they are considering an online degree, which further drives our orientation as a problem-solver for our constituents.

By answering these questions, we help any student interested in an online degree, not just those who will select the Walton College. It makes potential students aware of our program, but it also helps them know if our program is right for them. We don't use marketing to get *any* student into our programs; we want to get the students who are the best fit. We don't want trickery as any part of our marketing strategy or tactics.

The third category, thought-leadership blogs, has two subcategories—those based on research or peer-reviewed academic journals and those that don't involve a high level of academic rigor. For instance, we created a blog based on a podcast interview I did with an adjunct professor that was all about what it means to have an entrepreneurial mindset. It wasn't based on research, but the opinions and ideas qualified as thought leadership.

The members of our Marketing Advisory Board provide us with helpful advice on marketing. They also promote our content on their platforms, and, perhaps most importantly, they contribute content for the research-based thought-leadership blogs. These faculty members often publish books or academic articles. Peer-reviewed academic journal articles are primarily targeted to other researchers. This is how theory is built. Researchers take the refinements of theories or new theories, empirically test them, and continue refining them. In some disciplines, the literature reviews are lengthy and tedious and would not be of interest to most students, alumni, or practitioners. Some disciplines use complex statistics and probabilistic methodologies that take years to learn and understand. Other disciplines use deductive mathematical methods to prove theorems, propositions, and lemmas.

What we needed was a repeatable process that would take this type of research and turn it into short blogs that summarized the key findings in an interesting and actionable way for students, business leaders, or faculty who aren't experts in the same field.

The faculty, however, are not incentivized or rewarded for taking their published peer-reviewed articles and turning them into blogs. It's not a common practice, and the faculty were rightly concerned that this would add significantly to their workloads. So we came up with a process, with their help (which is procedural justice in setting direction), that eased those concerns.

The solution, which took us about a year to develop, was to use student interns who work for Modthink and students and staff in our Business Communication Lab (BCL), which provides proofreading services for Walton College students and helps them improve their communication skills. The interns and the student tutors from BCL, with the direction and approval of staff and faculty members, do the heavy lifting of repurposing the content toward the new audience. This makes it easier on the faculty members, while adding value to the learning experience for the students and value from the content for the audiences who read the blogs.

I wrote the first thought-leader blogs we produced for Walton Insights. I was the guinea pig until we worked out the kinks in the process. We also realized that I needed to put my money (or at least my time and energy) where my mouth is as a leader. I'm convinced that when an organization is implementing a novel process with strategic importance, the leader's actual engagement in the process helps others accept the process (gaining alignment).

Beyond that, writing regular blogs helps me achieve all the things I need to do as a leader. It is a great aid in setting direction, gaining alignment, and providing motivation around any message a leader needs to communicate. It is part of how a leader should be relating to people, casting vision, inventing, and sense making. It's a mechanism, for instance, for sharing information, encouraging people, and recognizing others for their achievements and successes.

When trying to decide if I should write blogs, I made a list of reasons why it would help me lead. Naturally, I wrote a blog about it: "21 Reasons a Leader Should Write Blogs," which was published on our Walton Insights website.

Videos and podcasts. I periodically record a podcast or video interview with our subject matter experts, and sometimes these recordings are repurposed as a blog or part of a blog. Doing this is part of an omni channel strategy, and I believe podcasts are particularly useful in this regard. Creating a transcript from a podcast is easy to do with today's technology. That transcript can then be used to create a blog or a post on social media or an email to a specific constituent group.

Since 2018 when we launched the Be Epic Podcast, we've released more than one hundred episodes. In addition to the SMEs on our Marketing Advisory Board, I have interviewed faculty, staff, administrators, alumni, benefactors, business leaders, and authors about business-related topics that connected back to our EPIC values.

I have enjoyed listening to podcasts for many years, and I had been a guest on them from time to time, but I had no experience creating a podcast when we purchased a voice field recorder. I'd never even heard of a voice field recorder! But suddenly I was using it to record interviews while meeting with people during my travels or when I could schedule an interview in my office. Sometimes I met with guests at the studios of KUAF, the local public radio station.

We began publishing the podcasts once a week on Wednesdays. After about six months, we paused to evaluate their effectiveness. We had published twenty-nine podcasts at that point, but we had several more in the editing and production stages.

The professionals at KUAF helped us greatly improve the technical quality of the podcasts. For instance, they asked me to connect lapel microphones to my field recorder so we would have higher quality sound and so they could equalize the volume of my voice with the volume of the person I was interviewing. They also helped us record new intros and outros, provided the editing services, improved the quality of our music, and helped me refine the structure we used for the flow of the interviews.

We also developed a well-thought-out and documented process for producing our podcasts, which made them easier to improve, redesign, and maintain. My role is to select the guests, conduct a pre-interview, and then record the podcasts. Seven other people handle tasks like scheduling, producing, reviewing, creating graphics for the posts, getting transcripts created and repurposed, uploading the podcasts and blogs, and promoting the content.

Unlike podcasts, video interviews weren't originally part of our marketing strategy. I began recording these interviews in Fall 2017 because I was looking to increase the amount of external input we were getting on entrepreneurship, which is one of our three strategic endeavors. The interviews were a way to get input from my newly formed Dean's Roundtable of Entrepreneurs and Market Makers (DREAM).

I wound up conducting video interviews with sixty Arkansas entrepreneurs. There were days when my entire schedule was booked with half-hour slots for these interviews, and they all provided great insights for me as dean of the business college. In addition, they turned out to be a boon to our marketing efforts. They gave us insight into problems we could solve for entrepreneurs, our students, our faculty, and many other constituents. We edited and began posting the videos in early 2018. We also transcribed the interviews, and we repurposed some of that content, as well.

Podcasts and video interviews are a salient part of our omni-channel marketing strategy. The pre-interviews and interviews help us empathize with our constituents, which helps us better understand and solve problems they might face. And, of course, the interviews are rich with content that provides practical solutions, helpful insights, and inspiring stories that provide value to students, faculty, business leaders and anyone else who listens to them.

Some of the interviewees serve as role models to students and encourage them to believe they can achieve similar things. And podcasts and videos sometimes help constituents network with one another, because they hear it and then reach out to the interviewee because of a common interest or for other reasons.

Partnerships. The Walton College is a big piece in a larger puzzle that also has smaller pieces vital to our mission. All these pieces need to fit together and work together in their marketing efforts. We need to make sure our marketing efforts work seamlessly to support the university's efforts, and we need our departments, outreach centers, labs, and studios to support our overall marketing efforts.

For instance, as were getting the Walton College marketing efforts off the ground, I began working more closely with our leaders at the McMillon Innovation Studio and the Brewer Family Entrepreneurship Hub. These are two unique assets that add great value to our students and the community, so it's important that they have a first-class web presence and communication that's consistent in what is said, how it's said, and how often it's delivered.

Their leaders needed visibility into the Walton College marketing plan, and my marketing team needed visibility into theirs. I wanted everyone aligned and supporting each other in ways that made sense and helped each other achieve their specific goals.

Events. In addition to inbound marketing (blogs, podcasts, website pages, etc.) and outbound marketing (advertising, promotions, etc.), the Walton College hosts several events that serve as components in our overall marketing strategy. The biggest of these are the Arkansas Business Hall of Fame ceremony, our Business Forecast Luncheon, and our Health and Business Symposium.

The Hall of Fame ceremony honors business leaders who have achieved significant success over their lifetimes. Their stories provide wonderful insights others can use, while inspiring us all to reach our own dreams. The forecast luncheon provides thought-leadership insights into the trends of the marketplace, which adds value by helping leaders build or adjust their strategies. And the symposium is a half-day event that brings together business, healthcare, and government leaders from around the state. It delivers value by giving these leaders a forum to discuss the future of healthcare and how the new digital health infrastructure can help the state's leaders build a healthier and more productive workforce.

Creating Unity

One of the best things about our improved approach to marketing the Walton College of Business is that it's not just about the Walton College.

Marketing, by nature, is a collaborative effort. It involves bringing diverse groups together to create and execute successfully. For us, that means reaching out to faculty, staff, students, business leaders, community leaders, and government leaders. It also means reaching out to leaders throughout the university. We're able to include them in the work we're doing, which helps them market their work and helps the university strengthen its incredible overall brand.

Academic institutions have a tendency to be territorial, but focusing on marketing—looking to solve problems for your customers and not protect your turf—is the antidote for territorial silos. Teams inside Walton College, around the UA campus, and across our network of leaders can work to understand the desires and feelings of customers, seeking to solve their problems and helping them seize opportunities. With the broader perspective of marketing, territorialism goes away because it is so obvious that it doesn't help advance the marketing cause.

When we do work together, we provide value while promoting our values. That's marketing.

(Note: If you're interested in how our approach to marketing fits within my leadership framework, see Appendix D.)

CHAPTER 10

Roadmaps: Structures, Strategies, and Priorities

I was in college when I came across a story by motivational author Zig Ziglar that still reminds me of the importance of establishing a clear destination as a leader.

In *See You At The Top*, Ziglar used Howard Hill as an example. Maybe you've never heard of Hill, but he once was extremely famous as an archer. In fact, in the 1930s through the 1950s, he was billed as "the World's Greatest Archer," and with good reason. He won a record 196 consecutive bow-and-arrow tournaments. He also performed trick shots all around the country, and was in several movies and short films. He even had a cameo part in *The Adventures of Robin Hood* (the uncredited role of Elwyn the Welshman). You might remember the scene where Robin Hood (Errol Flynn) splits the arrow of his competitor. Hill was the one who actually made that shot.

Under the right circumstances, however, Ziglar pointed out that most reasonably healthy adults could consistently shoot an arrow more accurately at a target than Hill—even with little to no experience with a bow and arrow. How? Blindfold Hill and spin him around ten times before he shoots, Ziglar said. Then Hill wouldn't be able to see the target, would have little idea where it was, and, thus, he would most likely miss it.

Ziglar's point: "If Howard Hill couldn't hit a target he couldn't see, how can you hit a target you don't have?" (Ziglar 1982).

Ziglar was writing to individuals, but his example applies to organizations, as well.

The mandate is our target at the Walton College, and the structure, strategy, and priorities help us hit it. If those are missing, poorly created, or misunderstood, then we become like the family I know who once made a four-hundred-mile drive to Nebraska to visit friends over the Christmas holidays. Their minivan was loaded with their four children, luggage, and gifts, and they were tired from the long ride when they arrived around

11:30 p.m. on a bitterly cold late December night. After ringing the doorbell several times without a response, they called their friends.

"We're here," the husband said.

"Where?" the friend responded. "I don't see you."

A few seconds later, they figured out the issue: The GPS had directed the family to the wrong house.

Developing the right strategies, providing the right structures, and keeping everyone aligned on the right priorities helps ensure we arrive at our desired destination, not some random home in the wrong neighborhood. If we just create the vision, mission, and values and put them in a book and walk away, which most actually people do, our probability of getting there is really low. People will go in all different directions.

Clarity around structures, strategies, and priorities is particularly important for a college dean, because faculty members are very independent. They choose their own research directions, and they set their own syllabi. The brutal reality is that some faculty members won't operate in ways that align with and support the mandate of the college. They were hired for a reason, of course, and maybe that reason is good enough to consider them an exception who doesn't need to pull on the main rope with the rest of us. The work they do might be tangential to what we're doing as a college, but it might not be. It would help everyone if they took part, and we want them to take part, but sometimes they refuse because . . . well, they can.

For those who want to help achieve our common goals, providing sound structures and clearly communicating strategies and priorities shows them the way. We make a lot more progress that way. Let those who say no, say no. But some people like to be on a team. Give them a way to do it. And when you get some momentum, even the naysayers usually start to contribute more. Those who are on the fringes—the small set of tenured professors who prefer to exist on the edges—are more likely to participate in some constructive ways when they can ride an existing wave.

To create this momentum, I've found that a dean must make sure that everyone within the college understands the structures, strategies, and priorities; is aligned to them; and is motivated to execute with excellence. The structure provides the ground rules on how the college operates. The strategies provide the roadmap for getting where we're going. And the priorities provide the focus that keeps us on the right road.

Let's look more closely at each of those and how my framework applies when leading in these areas.

Structure

The operating structure of a college supports its key initiatives and opportunities. If faculty and staff members are unclear about how the college operates, they will be confused about how to execute the strategic initiatives and priorities, even if they are fully on board with them. Thus one role of the dean is to help create an operating structure that works best for the college and regularly communicates key aspects of that structure to everyone involved.

For instance, in 2016 we began making changes to our organizational structure that included finding two new associate deans: one for academic programs and research and the other for executive education and outreach. So, I sent an email to the faculty and staff explaining the search process. I told them who was on the search committee, the timeline for applicants to supply information, and links to the job postings and descriptions. Then I provided the strategic context that explained what we were looking for in these new leaders and managers:

> For both of these positions, we need people who can delegate detailed budgeting and planning to the units while at the same time not abdicating the responsibility for budgeting and planning. They must ensure that budgeting and planning are occurring with excellence, and they must be able to share the results back to the executive committee and the rest of the college. These leaders need to make sure the units they are responsible for are making budgets and plans that are consistent with the overall direction of the college. Similarly, these two positions must be led by people who will delegate detailed organizing and staffing in their units while at the same time gaining alignment between the units and other units in the college (and sometimes with units outside of the college). Finally, these two positions must be led by people who can delegate control (making sure they are sticking to the plan and staying within budget) and problem solving while at the same time providing motivation to each of their units. In particular, I would like to see them motivate by (1) clarifying the mission to each of their units, and the roles their

units play in achieving the mission of the college, (2) getting their units involved in determining how they can help the college achieve its goals and objectives, and (3) recognizing accomplishments and caring for the people in the units. We don't need micromanagers in these positions.

The changes to our organizational structure continued into 2017. The associate deans communicated the details of changes within their respective areas, and I communicated the strategic changes.

We previously had an associate dean for research and graduate programs, an associate dean for undergraduate programs, and an associate dean for executive education. That structure, however, didn't facilitate alignment between undergraduate and graduate programs, let alone the adoption of best practices and taking advantage of common opportunities. So we changed all three associate dean positions.

The associate dean of executive education and outreach became responsible for executive education, the outreach centers, our McMillon Innovations Lab, and our Little Rock executive education initiative. And the associate dean of academic programs and research took responsibility for the Graduate School of Business, undergraduate programs, and the technology center. The other dean position became the senior associate dean with the role of aligning or realigning programs and processes across the college in a manner consistent with our vision and mission.

The senior associate dean straddles the strategic and operational functions of the college, reporting to me and overseeing the execution of strategy. The position also leads operations related to academic programs (through the associate deans and department chairs) and support functions. Among other responsibilities, the senior associate dean nurtures new initiatives and partnerships and continuous improvement initiatives, two elements that were clearly missing in our old structure. That change has made an enormous difference in the college's operations.

We also made changes to the responsibilities of assistant deans and transitioned to a centralized administrative team within the outreach and executive education department. The objective of this change was to streamline our processes, enabling our administrative roles to be more focused, efficient, and effective. This large and sweeping change called for identifying and including the right people in the decision-making process and communicating the process and the changes to those who would be affected.

At the beginning of the 2019–20 academic year, we rolled out additional changes to the structure of the dean's office. The biggest change involved our reporting structure—the proverbial org chart. In our old model, I had fifteen direct reports. That was too many, especially in light of the strategic development initiatives that were taking up a huge chunk of my time. Now the department chairs report to the senior associate dean (Anne O'Leary-Kelly).

We made several other changes to the reporting structure and responsibilities of the associate deans, then communicated them in an email that not only covered what was changing but why. We listed the initiatives that were taking up my time and making me less accessible to department chairs. We highlighted some of the credentials and experiences that made Anne more than qualified to oversee the work of the department chairs. And we outlined the other changes that affected our top leaders within the college. We also put together a one-page document for the department chairs that outlined the issues they should bring to Anne—things like policy questions, requests for additional staff, performance reviews, and compensation and promotion issues. The document also noted the issues where I still needed to be involved, like signing certain forms, writing promotion and tenure letters, and making the final decisions on promotions and tenure.

My advisory boards are another important part of our structure. The Dean's Alumni Advisory Council (DAAC) serves as ambassadors of the Walton College, helps us with planning, and generally looks for opportunities that will help us succeed in our mission. The Dean's Executive Advisory Board (DEAB) is committed to identifying strategic opportunities for students, strategically connecting faculty and industry, advancing and supporting our goals and strategies, and participating in fundraising activities. And the Dean's Roundtable of Entrepreneurs and Market Makers (DREAM) provides external input on one of our key strategic endeavors—entrepreneurship.

The DAAC, DEAB, and DREAM are invaluable advisors who help shape our future. For example, during one 2019 meeting of the DEAB, the members split into three groups and each group tackled a different question. One group made recommendations on our graduate program, helping us decide where to add new master's degrees. One group made recommendations regarding our Leadership Walton experience, a professional development program for undergraduate business students. And one group made

TYPE OF ACTIVITY

	ENGAGEMENT — Interactions with the target audience	INNOVATION — Knowledge creation that is relevant to the target audience	IMPACT — Knowledge/expertise that is used by the target audience
ACADEMIC — Other Scholars, Research Literature, The Profession	*Sample Activities* • Involvement in department or college research activities • Attending scholarly conferences • Conference paper presentations • Visiting scholar presentations • Journal reviews • Building research collaborations • Submission of papers to journals **1**	*Sample Activities* • Peer reviewed publications • Publishing Scholarly book • Attaining external funding for research **2**	*Sample Activities* • Citation counts • Editorial board for academic journals • Leadership roles in professional associations • Best paper awards • Fellow Status (or other designations) that reflect scholarly expertise • External reviewer for promotion and tenure at another university **3**
PEDAGOGICAL — Students, Other Teachers	*Sample Activities* • Effective teaching (undergraduate, masters, PhD) • Teaching-related presentations • Teaching-related mentoring • Involvement in curriculum design • Service on dissertation committees **4**	*Sample Activities* • Significant teaching innovations • Innovative efforts to integrate research and teaching • Innovative efforts to integrate practice and teaching • Writing textbooks • Creation of significant instructional materials or methods • Significant innovation in course design • Leadership in curriculum **5**	*Sample Activities* • Publishing with a doctoral student • Strong placement of doctoral students • Teaching or mentoring award • Leadership in teaching association • Leadership in College or University teaching center or program • Outstanding teaching evaluations • Editorial board for teaching journal **6**

PRACTICE		Sample Activities	Sample Activities	Sample Activities
	Practitioners	• Delivery of Exec Education programs • Involvement in outreach centers • Participation in professional association • Professional development activities • Engagement in consulting activities with external partners • Invited presentations to professional audiences • Internship with external organizational partner • Sustained professional work	• Development of new Executive Education programs • Collaboration with external partners in data collection • Publication in practitioner journal • Attaining research funding from industry sources • Attaining access to data from external partners	• Editorial board for practitioner journal • Leadership in professional association • Award from professional association • Application of innovations to business practices • Media citations • Attaining Patents • Invitation to collaborate with external partners to address societal issues
	Industry			
	Community			

The Process Used to Develop this Document

- For each of the Faculty Categories (SA, PA, SP, IP), the Research Committee developed a list of activities, which demonstrate that an individual is qualified to be on the faculty in the Walton College.
- The Executive Committee (EC) discussed how to assess faculty in relation to these activities. The EC reviewed approaches at peer institutions. We decided in favor of a narra-tive approach, as opposed to a point-based system, for several reasons: 1) The point system does not provide a rich consideration of faculty contributions; 2) the narrative system better fits our culture (given our strong industry ties and our varied types of faculty, we want to fully understand and recognize the contributions of each person).
- These activities were used by a subcommittee of the EC to develop the framework that links each faculty category to the expected activities of this faculty type.
- The Executive Committee ratified this Faculty Qualification (FQ) document in January 2015.
- The Department Chairs shared this FQ document with each faculty member in Spring 2015, around the time of the annual performance review.

Table 10.1. Walton College Faculty Qualification Grid

The Primary Focus of Faculty in Each AACSB Category

AUDIENCE	TYPE OF ACTIVITY		
	Engagement	Innovation	Impact
Academic	1	2	3
Pedagogical	4		
Practice			

"Scholarly Academics (SA) sustain currency and relevance through scholarship and related activities. Normally, SA status is granted to newly hired faculty members who earned their research doctorates within the last five years prior to the review dates." Faculty in this category will primarily focus on cells 1 and 4 in initial career stages and, over time, also perform activities in cell 2 and subsequently cell 3.

	Engagement	Innovation	Impact
Academic	1		
Pedagogical	4	5	6
Practice	7	8	9

"Practice Academics (PA) sustain currency and relevance through professional engagement, interaction, and relevant activities. Normally, PA status applies to faculty members who augment their initial preparation as academic scholars with development and engagement activities that involve substantive linkages to practice, consulting, other forms of professional engagement, etc., based on the faculty members' earlier work as an SA faculty member." Faculty in this category will primarily focus on cells 4 and 7 in initial career stages of being a PA and, over time, also perform activities in cells 5 and 8, and subsequently cells 6 and 9.

	Engagement	Innovation	Impact
Academic	1		
Pedagogical	4	5	6
Practice	7	8	9

"Scholarly Practitioners (SP) sustain currency and relevance through continued professional experience, engagement, or interaction and scholarship related to their professional background and experience. Normally, SP status applies to practitioner faculty members who augment their experience with development and engagement activities involving substantive scholarly activities in their fields of teaching." Faculty in this category will primarily focus on cells 4, 7, and 1 in initial career stages and, over time, also perform activities in cells 5 and 8, and subsequently cells 6 and 9.

AUDIENCE

"**Instructional Practitioners (IP)** sustain currency and relevance through continued professional experience and engagement related to their professional backgrounds and experience. Normally, IP status is granted to newly hired faculty members who join the faculty with significant and substantive professional experience as outlined below." Faculty in this category will primarily focus on cells 4 and 7.

AUDIENCE	TYPE OF ACTIVITY		
	Engagement	Innovation	Impact
Academic			
Pedagogical	4		
Practice	7		

Notes:

- In the first column, the text within quotes is based on AACSB standard 15 (see Eligibility Procedures and Accreditation Standards for Business Accreditation, Updated January 31, 2016 available at www.aacsb.edu/accreditation/standards).

- The shaded cells indicate the activities on which individuals in each category should primarily focus. The other cells are not shaded and the corresponding cell numbers are excluded.

- Numbers in cells match those in the Grid (previous page), and may be used to identify the activities on which individuals in each category should focus.

- **Decreasing darkness of shading** indicates how an individual's primary activities might progress as (s)he gains seniority and expertise. Thus, the darkest shaded cells (1, 4, or 7, depending on faculty category) are where an individual might focus in the early career stages while the less darkly shaded cells indicate how the individual's academic and professional engagement might change over time.

**Walton Faculty Qualifications
Grid for AACSB Purposes**

Table 10.1. (*Continued*)

recommendations for our executive education program. All three groups came up with at least one recommendation that we implemented within weeks of the meeting.

Our strategies as a business college also are shaped by the expectations of our industry. So in that regard, our accreditation from the AACSB, the gold standard for business and accounting programs, forms a key part of the structure that sets our course as a college. Fewer than 5 percent of business schools worldwide hold AACSB accreditation. Earning and maintaining it requires a rigorous review every five years.

It takes a great deal of time and energy on the part of our staff to prepare for these reviews, but the accreditation standards help shape our strategy. For instance, the accreditation involves three "pillar" components—engagement, innovation, and impact. As a result, we developed and adopted what we call the "faculty qualification grid" that outlines how faculty provide excellence for the three pillars (table 10.1). The process of creating that structure generated healthy discussions around faculty classifications and caused us to think carefully about the career journeys of our faculty, their development, and the value each classification of faculty provides to the college. And, of course, the detailed structure provides guidance for our faculty.

We continually evaluate ways we can improve the grid and use it more effectively. Right now, each of our departments use it as both a reporting tool and as a development tool.

Because we need structures that help us meet the accreditation standards, it's important that the faculty and staff commit to the process and understand its value. I explained this to our college in the summer of 2016 because we were scheduled for the review process in February 2017 and I wanted everyone to approach it with the right mindset.

The first benefit I mentioned was the obvious impact on the student body, because so many companies only recruit from AACSB accredited programs. But our students, faculty, and staff also benefit as a result of the accreditation process. For instance, the Continuous Improvement Review (CIR) process helps strengthen our engagement with business and industry, innovation in education and research. It also improves our teaching and student learning, research, connection to the world of practice, community involvement, and the demonstrated result of our centers.

In addition, the CIR process is an impetus for monitoring our progress over the previous five years, which helps us identify where we were strong and where we needed improvement. The CIR team consists of seasoned and knowledgeable deans and accounting department chairs from peer or aspirant schools who conducted multiple reviews each year. Therefore, the CIR process can offer invaluable advice about best practices and about ways we could improve.

Preparing for the 2017 review provided us with an opportunity to celebrate some of our successes in implementing our strategy and double-down on our efforts in areas where we were coming up short of our goals. I was able to share a letter from the AACSB affirming our success in the 2013 CIR process. They commended us on seven strengths, and specifically mentioned how our outreach centers were a "very effective best practice" that demonstrated significant accomplishments relative to each of the three pillars—engagement, innovation, and impact. This feedback directly supported our strategic decision to centralize the outreach centers and put them under the guidance of an associate dean.

The AACSB letter also included items where we needed additional focused attention for continuous improvement, so I was able to share with our faculty and staff what those were and how we were addressing them through our various new structures and strategic initiatives.

Strategy

The Walton College is one of ten colleges or schools at the university, and obviously we don't exist in a vacuum. So, our strategic plan must fit within and complement the strategy and vision of the university and its other academic units. As dean, my role is to help the Walton College create a strategy that aligns with the university's, to clearly and consistently communicate that strategy, and to ensure we're executing on it and getting the results we need.

Our current strategic plan was completed in October 2016 based on input from faculty, staff, students, and others that was gathered from task force committees and during town hall meetings. But it is an evergreen document. We're always in the process of evaluating it and improving it, not just for the sake of change but only when we find opportunities for meaningful adjustments based on new information and changing circumstances.

Every year, my executive committee has an offsite meeting where we address our strategic direction, which is how we create and align on a fresh approach to our plan. We typically do this with one off-site meeting, but in 2020, because of the pandemic, we did it with three video-conference sessions. During the first, we reviewed the results of a survey that told us how students rated our handling of three topics: COVID-19, academic quality, and diversity and inclusion. The second session focused on trends within the departments that were relevant to the entire college. And the third focused on next steps to take advantage of opportunities for the college in light of trends and student feedback.

Good strategic planning is an ongoing process that allows for changing circumstances and supports implementation of the best, most relevant ideas. I meet with our three associate deans each week, and we periodically discuss strategies, objectives, and measurable goals related to the strategic plan. This is important for implementation, because as we discuss the agendas, we also identify roadblocks to implementation and then we help one another overcome the roadblocks. Continually evaluating where we are and how we are performing helps us know when it's time to pivot.

President Dwight D. Eisenhower said, "Plans are useless, but planning is indispensable."[11] That's because planning helps us think through the details of where we want to go and how we will get there. But you can't just follow a plan blindly. We are always receiving new information about what is working and what is not working, as well as about new opportunities that we could not have anticipated.

So communicating the strategy is never a one-and-done event. I'm constantly reinforcing the established strategy, sharing details about changes, or emphasizing why it matters.

In addition to updates about our strategy throughout the year, I regularly share our plan overview. For instance, I send out a "Happy New Year!" email each January that thanks the faculty and staff for their work during the previous year and outlines why I'm optimistic about the year to come. That email typically covers six or seven items, and one of them is always our strategic direction.

---

11. Quoted in Six Crises (1962) by Richard Nixon and sited in The Columbia World of Quotations

On January 1, 2016, when I was still interim dean, I wrote the faculty and staff to say I was optimistic about these seven things:

1. Our new leader, Chancellor Joe Steinmetz
2. Our new hires in the Walton College
3. Our support from alumni
4. Our strategic direction
5. Our spirit scholars' program
6. Our momentum, based on the history of the Walton College
7. Our staff Six Sigma/Continuous Improvement Professional Development Program

It was a long email—more than two thousand words—and roughly one-third of it focused on item No. 4, our strategic direction. I pointed out that I had been involved in strategic planning processes for the college that were led by our three previous deans (Doyle Williams, Dan Worrell, and Eli Jones), that we currently operated using the plan developed under the leadership of Dean Jones, and that we were developing a new plan. I took some time to describe how we had come up with the strategic plan in the Spring 2013 during an off-site meeting at the headquarters of Tyson Foods. I then explained what we currently were doing with the strategic planning process, why it was important to individuals and to the college, and where we were going with it. I closed the email by reemphasizing the importance of aligning on values and direction.

Take a look at this lengthy excerpt from that email and you should see elements of the leadership framework I outlined earlier. As a leader, I was setting direction, aligning our team to a shared vision, and motivating them to take part. The primary capabilities involved in this communication were sensemaking, relating, and visioning.

We created a task force and held a series of meetings in which faculty and staff identified areas of strategic focus, using these to revise the mission statement so that it better fit AACSB's desire for a more specific and unique statement, and creating task forces to identify specific initiatives. Then we reported back to faculty and staff with the final initiatives and mission and vision statement. We are now in the process of giving our strategic initiatives more clarity, as well as measures, and we have done this by using task forces with the overall process organized and managed by Vikas Anand.

It is important for the Walton College to have a clear and measurable strategic plan for several reasons, including (1) it helps our college faculty and staff to be on the same page and understand where we are going, (2) it helps us make better and more consistent decisions, including the allocation of resources, (3) it contributes to the purpose and meaningfulness of our work, and (4) it helps our benefactors understand how they can provide resources to achieve our goals. There will be Town Hall meetings in February, March, and April to continue this process. I want to emphasize that Vikas and the task forces are actually working to set up metrics and evaluations of our existing strategic plan, not developing a brand-new plan.

Our values (excellence, professionalism, innovation, and collegiality) were created in the 1990's under Dean Doyle Williams leadership. We will also be clarifying and measuring how well we are doing in terms of living up to our values, again using a task force and other meetings. It is important that we make sure everyone understands and buys into our values, especially since we have a faculty governance to design and implement policies and procedures. Faculty governance is by its very nature decentralized and therefore our values must be understood and agreed to throughout our organization. (It is easy to remember our values if you remember that our values are EPIC—Excellence, Professionalism, Innovation, and Collegiality.)

What is our direction? We are moving in the direction of fulfilling our vision, and mission, living up to our values and becoming more self-sufficient through entrepreneurial endeavors. (When I talk about the Walton College being entrepreneurial, I'm talking about it as a unit. It is not that all of us need to be focused on entrepreneurial endeavors. Also, for those of us engaging in entrepreneurial endeavors, we must do so while excelling in teaching and research. We all have different strengths, capabilities, and interests, and this provides an avenue for our entrepreneurs to help us achieve our vision and mission in a way that is consistent with our values.)

How do we get alignment? We get alignment through communication, discussion, and engagement. If you have been reading the Executive Committee minutes or if you have been involved in one of our task forces, then you know that we are doing a lot in this regard, not just with strategic planning implementation but also with problem solving and with capturing opportunities.

We will all be better off if we are aligned on the strategic direction because we will be more likely to achieve it. We will have more resources. We will have more fulfilling work. We will have more impactful research. We will have more effective education. Our faculty, staff, students, benefactors, and other constituents will be better off. It is worth the effort and we can do it.

I sent a similar email at the start of 2017, again with seven reasons why I was optimistic about the future and with the longest section again covering strategic direction. Some of the content (the history and context pieces) were essentially the same, but this was necessary because new faculty and staff members had never heard the history and existing faculty and staff needed the reminder.

During my tenure as dean, we have added performance metrics and more tactics for implementation. In 2017, we created a number of new metrics and we posted them for the entire world to see on our website.[12] We created metrics to measure impact, and we organized the impacts around three audiences: academic audiences, pedagogical audiences, and practice audiences. In addition, we developed a category called "outcome metrics" for those impacts that either spanned all three or didn't fit well into one of the other categories.

Metrics for the impact on academic audiences measure originality of research, research leadership, visibility among peers, and duration of the impact. Metrics for the effect on pedagogical audiences measure the impact of teaching and recognition of teaching excellence, including these effects on other institutions. Metrics for the impact on practice audiences measure adoption of our thought leadership throughout the industry (figure 10.1).

The website features an icon representing each of the four impact areas. If you click on one of them, it shows you a number of metrics based on data from a rolling five-year period. We chose five years for two main reasons: (1) There can be lots of random variance within a given year, so five years smooths it out, and (2) AACSB reviews are every five years.

By clicking on the "academic" button, for example, you see that during a five-year span the Walton College had 542 publications in peer reviewed

---

12. https://walton.uark.edu/osie/reports/ic-impact.php

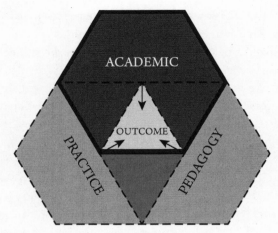

Figure 10.1. Intellectual Contribution Impacts
Source: https://walton.uark.edu/osie/reports/ic-impact.php

journals, 15,187 citations, 792 conference presentations, 127 best paper awards, 73 visiting scholar invitations, 66 editorial board memberships, more than $3 million in external funding of research, and 20 leadership positions in professional organizations. These eight metrics clearly measure the Walton College's impact on our academic audience.

Six metrics show up under the pedagogy button: 36 pedagogical publications, 132 teaching awards, 391 honors theses, 107 dissertations, 297 doctoral graduate publications, and more than 17,000 educational programs for K-12 Arkansas students.

There are eight metrics for the practice audience: 47 practice publications, 329 citations of our publications in the media, 2,500 people attended Walton College thought leadership events, more than 2,300 internships, more than 500 people went through our executive education programs, more than 40 business start-ups, No. 1 in the country in the number of student business plan competition wins, and more than 300 local jobs created through our small business center.

The outcome button has four metrics: an 88 percent placement rate, 388 business leaders on Walton College advisory boards, $143 million in philanthropy, and a 66.5 percent six-year graduation rate.

Now that we are collecting these metrics, we discuss them, open them up to the public, and make changes based on them. Making these metrics visible to the public creates accountability and more opportunities for interpretation. It improves alignment, provides motivation, and gives clarity about performance. It highlights what we are trying to accomplish, and it helps us know where we are succeeding and where we need improvement.

In addition, below the impact metric icon are hyperlinks for Engagement, Innovation, and Impact that take you to a list of articles published in the *Walton Today* newsletter. When our marketing team writes an article for *Walton Today*, they tag the article with one of these three titles. These aren't numerical metrics of performance, but they can be thought of as narratives on our performance in these three areas.

The metrics are an important way we evaluate the effectiveness of our strategy and hold ourselves accountable to it. They provide indicators for what we're doing well and where we need to improve.

In 2019, associate dean Brent Williams led the effort to review and update our strategic plan as part of our preparation for our AACSB accreditation. In addition to changes we might make to the actual plan, Brent began seeking input from faculty, staff, and administrators on how to improve our metrics so that they connected more directly to our mission and values, were easier to update regularly, and they provided more value to our daily decision making.

Priorities

There's an old illustration about setting priorities that involves pebbles, sand, rocks, and a glass jar. Two groups of people are given the exact same materials—the same size jars and the same amounts of the same-sized rocks, pebbles, and sand. Each group then is instructed to fill up their jars to the rim without going over, but they are given different instructions on how to go about it.

The first group must start with the rocks. For the sake of this example, we'll say the jar can hold six rocks. So, they put six rocks in, and the jar appears to be full. But, of course, the jar really isn't full. They can pour in the pebbles, which will fill in the spaces between the rocks. Again, it appears full. But, again, they can fill it even more with the sand.

The second group is instructed to start with the sand, then add the pebbles, and then the rocks. They end up using the exact same amounts of sand and pebbles as the first group, but they have room for only four of the rocks.

The rocks represent your top priorities, the pebbles your lower priorities, and the sand your lowest priorities. And the obvious point is that leaders and organizations should focus first on the biggest priorities or else those priorities will get squeezed out by things of lesser importance.

There's no shortage of great ideas at a business school. In fact, you'd be in big trouble if that weren't the case. A university should be filled with bright minds that originate creative ideas, both from within the faculty and the student body. That's certainly the case at the Walton College and throughout the University of Arkansas. Thus the question becomes, *Which ideas are the rocks, and which ones are pebbles or sand?*

The reality, for all leaders, is that we can't give our full attention to each idea that comes our way—even each very good idea. A dean is responsible for making sure that everyone within the college is focused first and foremost on the right rocks. That's not always easy because, as you know, we all have our pet rocks. And we really, really love our pet rocks. But all too often those pet rocks are the sand and pebbles that prevent us from collectively achieving our ultimate goals. So, while strategic planning is essential to the success of any organization, there's still the matter of knowing which rocks are the big-rock priorities and which ones are the pet rocks that need to live on a shelf.

Priorities help drive decisions about how resources are allocated, which directly affects the implementation of strategic plans. Some priorities never go away, but others change as goals are accomplished or as the needs of faculty, staff, and students change. So, evaluating, updating, and communicating priorities is essential to executing any strategy successfully.

Not long after I became dean, I had one of my first big opportunities to apply my framework to what's become an ongoing effort around priorities. Chancellor Steinmetz rolled out his eight priorities for the campus, and they represented a degree of uncertainty and change for some of our faculty and staff. We had just gone through a strategic planning process in the Walton College, so we had our strategic initiatives. But the faculty and staff weren't sure how the chancellor's priorities fit with our strategic planning process.

Leaders help people cope with change by setting direction, gaining alignment, and providing motivation, so it was my job to lead the college through this change. I made an intentional effort to keep our faculty and staff up to date on what was happening and why, both because I knew they'd want to be informed and because I wanted them to share my enthusiasm for the results the process would have on our work.

I used sensemaking by communicating things like, "The university's priorities help us prioritize the strategic initiatives that come out of our strategic plan." That makes total sense.

The visioning part involved painting the big picture by pointing out that we were all going to be better off with the entire campus aligned around the chancellor's common vision.

Inventing came into play because I had to figure out and then communicate how we would execute on the chancellor's priorities.

Relating was key to gaining buy-in. Individual professors, for instance, needed to know how the changes would impact their day-to-day lives. I was able to show them that following this process would make it easier for me, as the dean, to go to the chancellor or provost and secure resources for them to do research and get published. I knew what mattered to the professors because I could relate to their situations, and that helped me communicate to them the benefits of aligning on the shared vision.

My leadership team and I decided that as a college we would pick three priorities to emphasize. With the chancellor's support, we would drill deeply into those while not ignoring the others. When our strategic initiatives aligned with those three priorities and our mandate, then it gave us a green light to push for funding. This has guided our course ever since.

During my first two years as dean, our priorities focused on investing in faculty excellence, research, and diversity and inclusion. We did this by allocating resources toward several key needs, including salary increases, hiring new faculty, adding tenure track lines, increasing funds for research centers, labs, and travel for conferences, increasing stipends for doctoral students, and creating two new positions within our Office of Diversity and Inclusion (an associate director and an outreach coordinator).

In 2017, after making changes to our structure and to our Walton College strategic plan and with the chancellor's priorities for the university in mind, we began to reevaluate our college's priorities. I rolled the new priorities out during a faculty and staff meeting, but I set that meeting up with an email that explained where we were in the process and how we had gotten there.

Since new priorities need resources, one of the key points was to explain how we had funded our previous priorities. For instance, one of the ways we had secured more resources was through differential tuition—from $3 million in 2014 to $6.4 million in 2017. The increases were long overdue given the ROI on our degrees and the cost of running the college in a competitive manner. Differential tuition went from the fourth-largest source of revenue for the college to the second largest. Also, philanthropy went from 8 percent of our revenue to 10 percent during that time period. In all, we raised our budget by $5 million per year to help ensure we were well-resourced for our priorities.

I also gave a short overview of how we had arrived at the updated priorities for the execution portion of our strategic management plan. We had included input gathered over the previous two years from our internal strategic planning process, clustering information from things like the indicators and KPIs in our strategic plan, the priorities of the university, input from town hall meetings, and input from our advisory boards. We looked at how many indicators (developed in the strategic planning process) pointed to each of the overall campus priorities, as well as the overlap of our priorities and our strategic initiatives.

The next day at our faculty and staff meeting, I was able to reiterate these points to further create buy-in on the process and then detail the priorities in ways that built confidence in our reasoning for selecting them and in our commitment to pursuing them.

A week later, I used my weekly email (Messages from Matt) to recap the key messages from the faculty and staff meeting. Our top priorities for the next three years, I told them, were (1) achieving student success, (2) enhancing our research and discovery mission, and (3) reaffirming our responsibilities as the state's land grant and flagship university. I reminded people that these priorities would guide the implementation of our strategic plan, as well as resource allocation.

When rolling out priorities, it's important to create a sense of accountability. The faculty and staff needed to know that these weren't priorities that would sit idle—the dean's staff would be driving them. In this case, we assigned an associate dean to each priority—Anne O'Leary-Kelly took responsibility for our priority of achieving student success, Alan Ellstrand took ownership for our priority of enhancing our research and discovery mission, and Brent Williams took charge of our priority of reaffirming our responsibilities as a land grant and flagship university. Those associate deans then communicated specifics about what the priorities meant to the college.

In the following months, I was intentional about communicating our progress regarding both our strategic plan and our priorities. I continually reminded the faculty and staff where we were, how we got there, where we were going, and what progress we were making.

In early 2018, for instance, I wrote a series of messages to faculty and staff members. The first was an overview of the strategic planning process that brought us to where we were. Essentially, it was background and context that I'd shared several times before but that I wanted everyone to read again to reinforce that part of the message.

The next week I went over our three primary priorities as a college and how they fit within the guiding priorities for the campus that the chancellor established. Again, for many members of our faculty and staff, this was a message to reinforce what they should already have known. The third week I showed how the priorities connected to our strategy by using research as an example.

Research is listed in our strategic plan as the first initiative. Several of our top researchers in the college indicated that a research associate to help with statistics and database management for secondary data would help their research productivity. So, I pointed out that we were in the process of recruiting a research associate whose primary responsibilities would be data acquisition and data management for research projects focused on publishing scholarly work in leading academic journals. We would fund the position, I told them, primarily with money from our Supply Chain Management Research Center, with additional funding coming from Walton College outreach and executive education initiatives.

Implementing strategy within an organization requires resources, and our approach to strategic management includes using revenues generated by our outreach and executive education programs to support our research and teaching mission. So, I wanted our faculty and staff to see how our strategic management approach was helping us fund and execute our stated priorities.

When you look at the major initiatives we've launched since rolling out those priorities, you should see how they connect to our top priorities. Why did we give our freshman experience program a makeover? Because it helps us achieve student success. Why did we reduce teaching loads for top performing researchers? Because it helps us enhance our research and discovery mission. And why did we expand our executive education presence in Little Rock? Because it reaffirms our responsibilities as the state's land grant and flagship university.

By focusing on those big rocks, we made major strides in those areas, and we still had plenty of room for pebbles and sand.

CHAPTER 11

Our Vehicle: Research, Teaching, and Service

A 2019 job posting for the dean of the business school at a large university on the West Coast spent almost five hundred words outlining the responsibilities that came with the job and the qualifications of the ideal candidate. Not once, however, did it mention the word *research*—despite the fact that "research" was listed in both the vision and mission of the college the dean eventually would lead.

That posting was by no means the exception to the rule. Look at just about any job posting for a business school dean and you'll likely see something similar. And why not? Near the beginning of this book, I referenced a 2016 article in *The Chronicle of Higher Education* that pointed out how the dean of a modern business school no longer is just an administrator but also "part entrepreneur, part fundraiser, part marketer, and part seasoned administrator . . . with the ability to build partnerships and develop strong new programs capable of generating revenue" (June 2018).

Again, no mention of research. Nor, by the way, does it mention teaching. Or service.

Yet, every business college worth its mortarboards is responsible for research, teaching, and service. You might even recall that the Walton College begins its vision statement with those three roles: "Through our teaching, research, and service, the Sam M. Walton College of Business will be a thought leader and a catalyst for transforming lives in Arkansas, the United States and the world."

Research, teaching, and service are at the very heart of what we do as a college, so it stands to reasons that they must be a focus of my leadership as dean.

The Research Advantage

A dean, of course, isn't a researcher, at least not in the traditional understanding of that role. We don't spend time doing deep academic research with the intention of seeing it peer-reviewed and published. And deans often step into that office because they've focused more on administration than research. A background in research, however, has been a significant advantage for me in leading the Walton College of Business.

For starters, as I've mentioned already, research skills have come in handy when gathering information about trends, making decisions about strategy and direction, or getting to know donors and partners. There's a risk in getting over-analytical and becoming a roadblock to progress because you are too busy studying a problem to actually take the actions that might fix it. But more often than not, research skills have equipped me to lead and manage more effectively.

Another big advantage of a background in research is that it prepared me to help us live out our mandate. Research is essential to the University of Arkansas and the Walton College of Business. It's in our mission statement. It's in our priorities. It's the first initiative listed in our strategic plan, which says that, "a research college is a college that enables and motivates its members, including faculty and doctoral students, to conduct high-impact scholarly research, and rewards their successes in this arena." It's what we do and who we are.

My passion for research also strengthens my leadership credibility among professors. Research is a high priority for most faculty members at a research-based university, so they are more likely to support me as the dean if they feel confident that I'm committed to helping them pursue their research goals. Since I was a hard-core researcher as a professor, I brought that status and reputation with me when I was named dean. I still had to prove that it was important to me, but I was proving it from a position of strength.

Deans who were just average as researchers have to show that research matters to them. If the big-time researchers in the college think you're not leading them in a direction that's going to make the college better in terms of research, they're going to try to get you fired. So regardless of your background, make sure you support research if you are at a research university. You need to build your credibility in this area or people may think you're a good dean but that maybe you belong at a teaching school rather than a research university.

Research and teaching support each other at a research university, especially when you teach in the same area in which you do research. As an active researcher, you read new articles on the topic. You pay attention to what is going on in the industry on the topic. You engage in consulting on the topic. You build deep expertise and understanding in the topic. So when you teach that topic, you are up to date and can facilitate business cases effectively. Also, teaching on your research topic helps your research. It's true that "the best way to learn is to teach." As you teach a topic, you become aware of subtle nuances in the description and explanations of various phenomena.

As a dean with a research background, I'm inclined to be data-driven and to experiment. And as a business school professor and entrepreneur, I have been a student of leadership and management theories.[13] This book is an example of how my background in research and teaching has affected my leadership of the college. As dean, I have been using management and leadership theories and documenting my efforts and thinking about what is working and what is not working.

I emphasize research all the time in many different ways. You've no doubt noticed that thread throughout this book—whether I'm writing about marketing, fund-raising, communication skills, my approach to leadership, or just about any other topic, I almost always have examples that involve an emphasis on excellence in academic research.

Fortunately, the faculty in the Walton College are a big reason why the Carnegie Foundation for the Advancement of Teaching has classified the University of Arkansas as a "Research 1" institution every year since 2011, which means the UA is a doctoral university with "very high research activity." Only 130 of 4,424 public and private universities earned this classification, which puts the UA among the top 2.7 percent of colleges in terms of research activity. And research by Walton College faculty was cited nearly 25,000 times in 2018, according to Google Scholar data (table 11.1).

Part of a dean's role is to sing the praises of faculty who are excellent in research, encouraging them to continue that path of excellence and encouraging others to follow. But a dean must be more than a cheerleader.

---

13. The word *theory* is often used to mean an idea that is not realistic or not implementable. A strong theory, however, describes, explains and can predict phenomena. If you know good theory, it gives you an advantage in leading and managing.

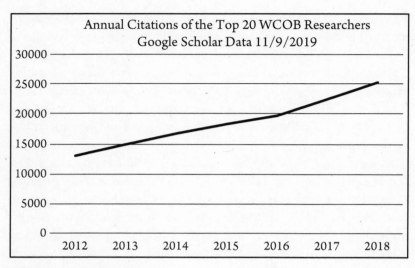

Table 11.1. Annual Citations

A dean takes action to make research possible. That happens in all sorts of ways—advocating for research centers, raising the funds necessary to operate those centers, putting money in the budget for resources, and creating a teaching structure that gives faculty time to do research and rewards those who do it well.

In 2019, for instance, I realized we needed to change the model we used for our faculty teaching load. We've long used a traditional 2/2 load model for tenure-track (TT)/Tenured (T) faculty, which means professors, associate professors, and assistant professors typically teach two classes in the fall semester and two in the spring. The rest of their time is devoted mostly to research and service (e.g., participating on university committees or working with PhD students). Hiring and keeping top professors, however, has become more competitive, and many of them prefer to spend more time on research and less time teaching. So we adopted a 2/1 model—two classes one semester, one class the next.

As you might expect, this decision was a hit with our faculty. But there was a downside. To make the plan work, we had to make sure that the professors actually were producing great research. So we decided to review the research production of our professors on a five-year rolling basis. Those who maintain a high level of research productivity get the 2/1 teaching load. Those who fall below a threshold of productivity for research move to a 2/2 or 3/3 load.

I knew this part of the change would be painful for some professors, including some who are my close friends. But I felt like it was just. To be a good fiduciary, I had no choice. We needed to give our top research professors more time for research if we were going to compete with other business colleges. And by shifting some professors to 3/3 load, we also could have smaller classes, which would help improve teaching quality.

I could have created and handed down this policy on my own, by the way. When I first became dean, I probably would have made the decision and then put together a committee to figure out how to implement it. Experience, however, taught me the value of making procedural justice part of the process.

We discussed it in our executive committee meetings, and the minutes from those meetings are shared with the college. I assigned Alan Ellstrand, our associate dean for academic programs and research, to lead the initiative, and he formed a committee to create a policy that we would socialize throughout the college. Then the executive committee would vote on the new policy.

The committee started with questions like, "What should be the teaching load for people who aren't highly productive in research?" Then they moved toward solutions on how to implement our new policy. I had my own answers in mind, but I realized the committee would either land in the same places I had landed or they would come up with something even better. And everyone in the college would know the decisions weren't made in a vacuum.

Learning from Our Best

One of the best ways to improve an institution's research excellence is to learn from those who do it best. So in 2019, we put together a "Walton College Research Team" that consisted of the most widely recognized, top researchers in the college.

This dream team consisted of researchers from the Walton College, including six of the top ten in the entire university—Scot Burton (marketing),

Varun Grover (information systems), Jon Johnson (management), Mary Lacity (information systems), Rajiv Sabherwal (information systems), and Viswanath Venkatesh (information systems). Then we brought in Blake Woolsey, one of the top facilitators in the country, to lead a discussion about best practices with a goal of designing a program to help our scholars realize their full potential.

In preparation, they were asked to consider the following questions:

- What do you believe has been a key driver to your success as a researcher?
- When you reflect on your research career, are there any specific experiences or people who helped along the way to help you excel and succeed?
- What have been lessons learned that you wish someone had shared with you?
- What would be your advice to a junior scholar (as well as a mid-career scholar) today who wishes to be a successful researcher? What are the top two to three priorities they should know?

When they met, the group divided into two smaller groups and focused on one question: What should the Walton College provide our researchers to help them be successful?

Their ideas were phenomenal. As I told them in an email after reviewing the results, "In my mind, you all scored a success here. I think your meeting was a milepost in the epic of the Walton College. Thank you."

They came up with about two dozen actionable ideas. And after the discussion, we moved forward immediately with four priority initiatives:

- Send out a survey to faculty to assess needs and current ways of working
- Host a similar facilitated session for junior and mid-career faculty to get their input
- Put together a brown-bag series using a broad spectrum of recognized research faculty to speak and help others in this space
- Build a webpage that pulls together all resources to help faculty with their research efforts

I was excited about these ideas because I could envision the positive impact they would have on our research efforts. Not only would they impact the ongoing research, but they would encourage faculty who had given up on research to get going again. They also would inspire a culture of continuous improvement around research.

Making Research Relevant

The value of academic research has come into questions throughout the ages. Some researchers have abused the funds they received and given the rest of us a black eye. And, most deeply, academic research can come across as overly dense to the general public precisely because it's written for an audience of experts on a topic, not the general public.

Johann Neem, an associate professor of history at Western Washington University, put it this way in an opinion piece for InsideHigherEd.com: "The purpose of academic scholarship is to engage in disciplinary inquiry— to further scholarly conversations. Such work will never be accessible to the general public since it, by definition, works at the boundaries of knowledge and takes a certain amount of prior knowledge and expertise for granted" (Neem 2014).

Publishing in academic journals contributes to faculty career success. And while academic articles are written for academic audiences, important research findings from business faculty often are abstracted in the *Wall Street Journal, Fortune, Business Week*, and other mainstream media. Articles often become textbook content.

At the same time, there's often a disconnect between academic research and industry practice, even though academic research has led to innovation and practical application. To help bridge that gap, deans need to emphasize and support this aspect of scholarship, as well.

I found this to be true before I became dean, because my research led to industry partnerships (and the founding of a company), as well as multiple opportunities for executive education that pushed researched findings out to practitioners. Some of our faculty members regularly consult with and partner with companies of all sizes all around the world. But this remains an area in which we can improve.

This is important not only to the practitioners who stand to benefit from research findings, but also to faculty members who benefit from partnerships with organizations they can study. So Jon Johnson, a longtime professor of management and now the chair of the Department of Strategy,

Entrepreneurship, and Venture Innovation, met with me in 2019 to talk through the ways the Walton College could make research more useful to business leaders. Johnson also is chairman of the Sustainability Consortium, and he is one of the top researchers at the University of Arkansas.

Here are some of the ideas the meeting generated:

- Identify individuals who have a vested interest and bring them together to listen to each other and educate them on opportunities.
- Create a list of research opportunities and distribute to the Dean's Executive Advisory Board (DEAB). Members can share and connect with those who might be interested.
- Identify the top ten corporations the Walton College wants to work with. Share this information with the DEAB so we can start to create connections.
- Encourage faculty to attend industry conferences (oil and gas, trucking, etc.) to get ideas of what problems they face. Academic institutions typically are represented at these conferences, so it is a potential competitive advantage.

The areas where we felt we had the most opportunities included blockchain technology, supply chain, and social problems (particularly research that helps alleviate poverty in southeast Arkansas).

Alan Ellstrand, the associate dean for academic programs and research and one of the top twenty researchers at the University of Arkansas based on the number of citations in Google Scholar, coordinated the meetings with the top researchers in the college. Having a successful researcher in his role is crucial to the success of the research function of the college.

Supporting the Team

When you buy vegetables from a street vendor along the gulf coast of Louisiana, chances are good that you'll get something you didn't pay for thrown into your bag—a few peppers, perhaps, or maybe some cilantro. They call it *lagniappe* (pronounced *lan-yap*), a Cajun word that means "a little something extra." The New Orleans *Times-Picayune* historically used *Lagniappe* as the title for somewhat random notes it published each day. The word is still commonly used in that part of the country to describe just about anything that's considered a bonus.

Added value, you might say.

When I communicate as dean of the Walton College, I find myself throwing in a whole lot of *lagniappe*—messages that add value by providing random bits of information that's useful, encouraging, or inspiring with regard to research, teaching, and service.

For instance, I often send out emails reminding our faculty and staff of events on the horizon—the last day of final exams, commencement ceremonies, holidays, banquets, panels, town hall meetings, business forecast luncheons, our Hall of Fame inductions, or fund-raising events. I might send an entire email about one of these topics (like the Hall of Fame, Martin Luther King Jr. Day, or our progress with accreditations) so I can provide context and background (sensemaking), or I might just throw in a bullet item in a list. Short items often carry big weight, like just noting the number of graduates who go through commencement.

The communication pieces also include things like new hires and promotions, which provide a good opportunity to sing the praises of our faculty and staff accomplishments, as well as on updates on initiatives we've started. These updates are good reminders that action actually follows the plans we announce.

One of the ways I relate to our faculty and staff is by letting them know I'm aware of the challenges they face and, when possible, by following up with ways to help them meet those challenges. This takes all sorts of forms, of course, but it begins with awareness, which goes back to listening. As leaders, it's often easy to hear what we want to hear and tune out complaints or even the concerns of those around us. By listening to understand, we often can help people make sense of their challenges and provide inventive solutions that help them succeed.

Listening to understand very often takes the form of asking questions that allow people to find solutions on their own as they explore the answers. Sometimes it comes by connecting them to other experts who can help. And sometimes it involves offering practical advice based on my experiences.

For example, it's important for our faculty and staff to tap into the people resources found all around our region. Executives, retired executives, business owners, and other practitioners are uniquely positioned to help us achieve our mission of advancing and disseminating business knowledge. But finding the right people for specific needs isn't always easy.

Committing to Service

Here's an interesting reality about people: They are willing to help you with just about anything if you are willing to ask. There's something honoring about having someone ask for your opinion, for your help on a project, or for your contributions in serving others. This goes back to my belief in practicing procedural justice in decision-making. I believe that by asking for input, people provide useful information and ultimately are more supportive of your direction and end up more involved in opportunities to serve the college and the community.

We also ask our faculty and staff to fill out questionnaires anonymously that provide us with feedback on things like what they need, how well they are connecting to our vision and mission, and how we're performing as leaders. And we ask them for ideas on topics we should discuss in our faculty and staff meetings, in our town halls, and in the emails sent by me and my leadership team.

Another way I ask our faculty for help is when we have openings for key jobs in the department. Our faculty and staff often are our best recruiters. They are among the best in their disciplines, and they know many of their peers who would fit into our culture and who would share our EPIC values. So at times I'll tell them about an opening and send them links to the job description and application.

I also regularly share opportunities for community involvement like how to become a mentor in the Big Brothers, Big Sisters organization, or how to volunteer for our annual Block Party to welcome and get to know students. This allows me to raise awareness about community needs and encourage our employees to serve others, which adds its own value to the Walton College.

Fortunately, we have a faculty and staff who naturally seem to gravitate toward acts of service, so my role often is simply to encourage and support the great ideas they bring to the table. They serve on college and university committees, they organize fund-raisers, they are editors of publications, and they launch initiatives from scratch.

In 2019, for instance, Professor Remko Van Hoek came up with the idea of giving the CSCMP Supply Chain Hall of Fame a physical home in northwest Arkansas. I gave him my support, but he did most of the work, and now the hall is open to the community. And during the COVID-19 crisis, our faculty and staff responded in many ways—from creating a webpage that supported area restaurants to spearheading a global collaboration to help bring much-needed personal protective equipment (PPE) to hospitals in the heartland.

It's important to recognize faculty and staff for their acts of service, and I'll cover that in more detail in a later chapter. But the first priority is to support and encourage service opportunities. If the opportunities don't exist or if people are discouraged from taking part, then they won't live out this important part of our vision.

CHAPTER 12

Reaping the Benefits of Diversity

When you walk in the lobby of the Reynolds Center for Enterprise Development, you can't help but notice that the back wall is lined with plaques honoring the members of the Arkansas Business Hall of Fame. You'll also likely notice that most of the photos on those eighty-eight plaques have at least one thing in common: they are of white males.

In fact, only ten members of the hall are not white males.

When I look at those tributes, I am in awe of the contributions those men and women have made by building strong, profitable businesses and giving back to their communities. Every one of them deserves to be in this Hall of Fame, and I am encouraged and inspired by the examples they've all set. But I'm also motivated to ensure the Walton College does what it can to develop and support diversity and inclusion in business so that a greater diversity of leaders can tap into their potential and perhaps one day find a place on that wall.

The low representation of women and minorities in the Arkansas Business Hall of Fame is a reality created by the past. One of the criteria for selection is that a candidate, if living, must be at least sixty years old. And the most successful business leaders of that generation, especially those who are Arkansans by birth or choice, happen to be white males.

That reality is changing with every passing year, however, and I consider it my responsibility and privilege to help champion that change by how we approach diversity and inclusion at the Walton College.

When I talk about diversity, by the way, I'm talking about the various differences humans bring to any group environment. You might add diversity to a group because of your race, your sex, your age, your religious beliefs, your cultural background, your socio-economic background, the state or country you group up in, your unique abilities or disabilities, or any number of other aspects of your life.

Inclusion, meanwhile, addresses the reality that we all want to feel like we belong—that we're included and valued as part of a group. We want to be proactive about creating a culture where people—students, faculty, staff, and anyone who visits our campus—feels respected and valued.

A commitment to that type of diversity and inclusion is hugely important to me for several reasons.

First, it is part of my mandate as dean. The mission of the Walton College challenges us to "advance and disseminate business knowledge using a diverse, inclusive, and global perspective." That alone would tell you we need students and faculty members who are as diverse as the world. Furthermore, enriching campus diversity and inclusion is a guiding priority in the University of Arkansas strategic plan, as well as one of the seven strategic initiatives for the Walton College.

Diversity and inclusion are particularly important to the University of Arkansas because it is both the state's land-grant university and its flagship university. That means we have a responsibility to serve the entire state. We also are the only true research university in the state, so it's even more important that we provide opportunities to a diverse population.

Second, it is relevant to the world in general and to businesses in particular. We live in a more diverse, connected world than ever, and one of our roles is to prepare students to succeed in that world. Think about this: J.B. Hunt Transport—a trucking and logistics company that does most of its business in the United States—has a workforce that speaks more than twenty-five different languages—just one of many measures of how diverse the typical workforce is in today's marketplace.

We want to teach students how to respect and honor people who are different not only because that's morally a good thing but also because it's a good best practice for a business. Research proves that diverse, inclusive organizational cultures produce innovation and strong financial results.

A 2017 study by the Boston Consulting Group (BCG) found that diversity on leadership teams increases the bottom line for companies. The study surveyed employees from more than 1,700 companies across eight countries. It found, among other things, that companies with more diverse management teams had 19 percent higher revenue due to innovation (Lorenzo, R., et al. 2018).

Katherine W. Phillips, a professor of leadership and ethics management at Columbia Business School, points out that "you would not think of building a new car without engineers, designers, and quality-control experts" (Phillips 2017). But after spending decades reviewing research from "organizational scientists, psychologists, sociologists, economists, and demographers," Phillips says the value of social diversity isn't always so clear-cut (Phillips 2017).

"Research has shown that social diversity in a group can cause discomfort, rougher interactions, a lack of trust, greater perceived interpersonal conflict, lower communication, less cohesion, more concern about disrespect, and other problems," Phillips said.

But the upside, she continues, is that, "Diversity enhances creativity. It encourages the search for novel information and perspectives, leading to better decision making and problem solving. Diversity can improve the bottom line of companies and lead to unfettered discoveries and breakthrough innovations. Even simply being exposed to diversity can change the way you think" (Phillips 2017).

The best way we can prepare our students to thrive in a diverse workforce and reap the benefits of diversity is to create a college that is diverse and inclusive.

Third, it is personal. As I mentioned near the beginning of this book, my faith informs my approach to leadership, and that faith places an immeasurable value on the inherent worth of all people. If there were no other reason than this, it would be more than enough to motivate me in this area.

No matter where you are as a leader, but especially if you happen to lead a business college, I believe you should emphasize the importance of diversity and inclusion, both in your personal leadership and in the ways your institution operates.

The Leader's Awareness

When you think about it, an awareness and understanding of diverse groups is essential to effective leadership. You can't gain alignment and provide motivation without that awareness and understanding. And your capabilities in sensemaking, relating, visioning, and inventing all are supported by a greater appreciation for the unique gifts, talents, insights, experiences, and perspectives that come from people who are different from you. (Appendix E shows an example of how this appreciation is filtered through my leadership framework.)

I'm challenged daily to look at the world around me with fresh eyes. That starts by acknowledging that my perspective is shaped by my ethnicity, sex, nationality, religion, how I was raised, where I was raised, the experiences I've had, and the friends I've made. These factors not only shape how I view the world but also how others view me. Next, I need to acknowledge that I don't know all the details about the factors that shape the people around me.

When I recognize these things, I'm better at helping others understand me, and I'm more eager to understand other people. I'm more forgiving and less judgmental, I make fewer false assumptions, I ask more questions, and I listen more thoughtfully.

I'm intentional about confronting my personal bias and broadening my perspective when it comes to diversity and inclusion. For instance, in 2019 I attended a leadership workshop in Boston that was specifically designed to help participants build skills related to diversity. In fact, the group that hosted the workshop is called, "White Men as Full Diversity Partners."

I also lean into our college's expertise. That includes the leaders in our Office of Diversity and Inclusion, of course, but also many other faculty and staff members. For instance, Anne O'Leary-Kelly, our senior associate dean, once came across a one-pager with advice on how to avoid gender biases when writing letters of recommendation. By sharing it with the college, she helped make us all aware of simple things we could do to write better letters—things like emphasizing accomplishments, not effort, and avoiding adjectives that invoke stereotypes. But she also helped us see our gaps and better understand other people.

By exposing myself to training, books, articles, and, most of all, people, I grow my personal ability to understand and relate to our students, faculty, staff, donors, alumni, and community members. That growth in my personal ability to relate to others helps me recognize where we need more diversity and inclusivity, while also helping me innovate solutions that will shape our future.

Strategic D&I

Because diversity and inclusion are pillars in our strategic plan, we have established goals around key indicators, and we measure our success. Right now, we are using three key indicators—awareness of diversity issues;

perception of safety to discuss issues related to diversity; and faculty, staff and students' sense of inclusion or belonging in the college. We measure our success against these indicators with surveys, external audits, and by tracking retention rates of minority students, staff, and faculty.

Every department within the Walton College has its own diversity and inclusion plan, and department heads regularly report to the executive committee to share what they are doing and the results they are seeing.

Quite simply, we know we need to recruit and retain more diverse faculty, staff, and students, while simultaneously ensuring everyone is treated with respect and fairness. If we fall short in one area, the other suffers. If we succeed, however, our college will look more and more like the increasingly diverse population of the United States.

When it comes to creating diversity on campuses, universities across the country have made more progress with recruiting minority students than with minority faculty in the past few decades. In 1995–96, for instance, 69.8 percent of undergraduates were white, according to a report by the American Council on Education. By 2015–16, 52 percent of undergraduates were white.

Almost every racial minority group increased in its share of enrollment during that time period, with Hispanics making the biggest jump—from 10.3 percent in 1995–96 to 19.8 percent in 2015–16. The non-white share of graduate students, meanwhile, grew from 20.8 percent in 1995–96 to 32 percent in 2015–16 (Espinosa et al. 2019).

Faculty members, on the other hand, remain largely white and predominantly male. In fall 2016, whites held 73.2 percent of the full-time faculty positions (Espinosa et al. 2019).

The UA tries to recruit a student body that mirrors the state's demographics, and in many ways we're successful. Arkansas is almost exactly 50 percent male and 50 percent female, and 53 percent of our student body are female. The state population, meanwhile, is about 72 percent non-Hispanic white and about 8 percent Hispanic/Latino, and roughly 76 percent of the UA student body is white and 8 percent is Hispanic/Latino.

In other areas, however, we have a good bit of work to do. Blacks, for instance, represent nearly 16 percent of the state's population, but less than 4.5 percent of the UA student population.[14]

---

14. The state population statistics are July 1, 2018, estimates from census.gov/ quickfacts/AR; the UA statistics are from the Spring 2019 11th Day Enrollment Report.

Arkansas is a small state and most of its 3 million people are clustered into a few urban areas. Nearly one-third of the state's population, in fact, lives in three of the seventy-five counties—Pulaski County in central Arkansas (which includes Little Rock) and Benton and Washington counties in northwest Arkansas (along the Interstate 49 corridor that runs through Fayetteville and Bentonville).

Blacks in Arkansas mostly live in the central, southern, and eastern parts of the state, so the flagship campus of the UA is not exactly in their back-yard. These potential students also tend to come from families that don't have many college graduates and that deal with generational economic challenges. For instance, the unemployment rate in Arkansas typically is double among minorities (in 2016 it was 3.3 percent for whites, 6.6 percent for minorities)

All of this means that we, as leaders at the UA, need to work hard to create opportunities for black students who desire a top-flight education. These opportunities benefit those students and their families, of course, but they also benefit the rest of our student body by adding unique experiences and perspectives, and they benefit the overall economy in our state.

In addition to recruiting a more diverse student body, we also must improve the diversity of our faculty. They not only serve as researchers and teachers, but as role models, and students need to learn from and appreci-ate a broad range of perspectives.

As dean, I need to make sure we're not just giving lip service to diversity when we make hires. I have told my executive committee to make sure we have and interview at least one diverse candidate in the candidate pool as we recruit faculty, for instance, because we can't hope to hire diverse faculty members if they are not in the pool of candidates we are considering.

To get a variety of candidates, we have to start well in advance of our official search by developing relationships with doctoral students or faculty who might consider coming to Walton in part because of the relationship we've built with them. We also need to develop a pool of homegrown tal-ent from our doctoral students. And we need to build relationships with affinity organizations that can help us find talented but underrepresented faculty members.

When the Department of Economics was recruiting a macroecon-omist, for instance, it posted the position with groups like the National Association for Hispanic Economists (as well as to groups of female economists and others that broadly represent minorities). The Department of Economics also put together a task force to review the diversity in its curriculum and made an effort to feature speakers with research interests relevant to minorities during research seminars.

The Culture Challenge

We can use many selling points when recruiting faculty and students to the Walton College—the highlights include the quality of our existing faculty and programs, strong financial support, and a region that's rated among the best in the nation for economic growth and quality of life. None of that matters much, however, if our culture isn't supportive of the different people we are trying to recruit.

College Factual, which ranks the diversity of a school by using metrics around variety in ethnicity, gender, age, and geographic location of origin, gives the University of Arkansas an overall score of 88.67 out of 100.[15] While that means the UA is "one of the most diverse schools in the nation," we're still not where we'd like to be when it comes to building and supporting a diverse student body.

The killing of George Floyd (who was black) by a Minneapolis police officer (who is white) in the early summer of 2020 was a tragic reminder of how far we have to go as a nation when it comes to racial and social justice issues. It caused many individuals and institutions to look in the mirror and acknowledge some difficult truths. The Walton College was no different.

One of the disheartening realities we faced as a college in the weeks following Floyd's death was some of the social media posts by minorities who had previously been silent about negative experiences during their time at the Walton College. While I was brokenhearted to learn of some of these experiences, I was thankful that they spoke up, because we needed to hear the truth. And we need to do more to make sure our culture improves.

As always, change begins with leadership. My role in shaping a more diverse and inclusive college is to lead by example and to provide the encouragement and support others need to co-create a future that aligns with our vision.

---

15. https://www.collegefactual.com/colleges/university-of-arkansas Last accessed January 18, 2021.

In short, I need to do all I can to help recruit a diverse faculty, staff, and student body, while also developing a culture that's inclusive and support-ive. I damage that mission when I, as a leader, don't surround myself with a diverse leadership team or when I fail to make every effort to listen to and learn from students, faculty, staff, alumni, and partners who are different from me.

I look for opportunities to address this priority with all my communica-tion efforts as dean, regardless of the audience or the mode of communica-tion. But one approach in particular that I've greatly enjoyed is my weekly Be Epic podcast. In 2020, for example, I interviewed:

- Nathaniel Burke, one of our black PhD students in economics, about his research on the effects of identity on decision making and how it informs us in recruiting and retaining underrepresented groups.
- Gerald Alley, founder and CEO of Con-Real, LP, a company involved in construction, real estate, and technology services and one of the nation's largest minority-owned businesses. Gerald was inducted into the Arkansas Business Hall of Fame in 2020.
- Dani Monroe, author of *Untapped Talent: Unleashing the Power of the Hidden Workforce*. Dani has had a lengthy career in diversity and inclusion, and now is vice president and chief diversity, equity, and inclusion officer for Boston-based Mass General Brigham, a health-care system with more than seventy thousand employees.
- Terry Esper, a black business school professor at The Ohio State University who is an alum of the Walton College.

I love hearing the stories of these men and women, learning from their insights, and sharing what they know with my listeners.

Another way I believe a dean can support diversity and inclusion in a business college is by making sure it has the right programs and policies in place and that the people running those programs have the support they need and a voice in decision-making.

The not-so-secret weapon of the Walton College is our Office of Diversity and Inclusion, which was founded in 1994 to "support, advocate, and assist" with "plans for diversity throughout the college."

Barbara Lofton, an assistant dean and member of the Walton College executive committee, has been the director since 1994. She has built an impressive and engaged advisory board that is helping us with the strategic direction of the college. She also has led our planning efforts for recruiting black and Hispanic students, creating a welcoming environment that promotes diversity and inclusion, and collaborating with and supporting various colleges to increase retention and graduation rates among minority students.

On January 18, 2021—Martin Luther King Jr. Day—we announced that an endowed scholarship had been created in Lofton's honor and that the department she leads was renamed the Dr. Barbara A. Lofton Office of Diversity and Inclusion.

We broke the news about these honors during a group Zoom meeting, and one of the participants was Gina Alley, a graduate of the Walton College and the daughter of Walton College graduates Gerald and Candace Alley.

"When I was in school," Gina Alley told Lofton, "you were literally the biggest champion for black students on campus—no matter what college they were in. You not only wanted us to excel. You cared" (Speer 2021).

Barbara's office offers a good many services and programs to students and to the overall community. In the summers, for instance, it runs a business leadership academy, a residential program for underrepresented incoming freshmen to learn about business majors while also developing leadership skills and support for the transition to college.

It also provides one-day camps on technology, both on campus and in central Arkansas, for students in grades six through eleven. In addition, it runs the Fleischer Scholars Program, a week-long summer program for rising high school juniors and seniors who are first-generation, low-income students with an interest in business. The program assists students in their preparation for college, and it also provides scholarships to applicants who are admitted to the UA, demonstrate leadership instincts and the ambition to succeed, and show a commitment to give back to the community through service.

The Walton College also hosts or cohosts a number of events throughout the year designed to promote diversity and inclusion among students, faculty, and staff. Each fall since 2014, for instance, we have held a Diversity and Inclusion in the Workplace Panel, where speakers discuss issues like the importance of diversity and inclusion in the global economy, the various ways in which their organizations recognize and value different perspectives and talents, and why that is vital to an organization's survival and growth. The 2019 event included panelists from Arvest Bank, General Mills, J.B. Hunt, and Walmart.

In Fall 2020, our newly created D&I Taskforce came up with the idea of a community book experience, which led to the development of "Let's Talk About Integrity and Race," a program that included a book discussions, workshops, and speaker series for students, faculty and staff of the Walton College. The Office of Diversity and Inclusion and the Business Integrity and Leadership Initiative cosponsored the program.

As a college, we read *So You Want to Talk About Race* by Ijeoma Oluo, who also was one of our speakers. The fourteen new members of our Walton College faculty that fall all got a gift box containing a copy of Oluo's book and an invitation to participate.

The taskforce also worked with faculty and the executive committee to come up with a diversity statement for syllabi. It is considered a living document, but here was the first version:

"The Sam M. Walton College of Business values the diversity of its students, staff, and faculty as a strength and critical to its educational mission. Walton College strives to be EPIC in our efforts to respect everyone, value our differences, and welcome all. We require every member of the Walton College community to contribute to an inclusive and respectful culture for all in its classrooms, work environments, and at campus events and to speak up in situations where this may not be occurring. It is our promise to provide our students, staff, and faculty with an intellectual community enriched and enhanced by diversity along a number of dimensions, including race, ethnicity and national origins, gender and gender identity, sexuality, class and religion."

Furthermore, all faculty members were given a copy of "The Inclusive Curriculum," an article in BizEd, and were asked to make at least one change to their courses (in addition to the statement in their syllabus). For instance, Business Law, a course all business school freshman take during their first semester, now includes curriculum on legal issues around discrimination and racism. The taskforce also came up with a corresponding micro credentialing process: a set of activities and achievements that will result in the issuance of a D&I badge that can be posted on LinkedIn.

All of these efforts, I believe, will make a difference. Over time, I am convinced we will make significant progress in creating a diverse and inclusive business college that produces alumni who will help create a more diverse and inclusive marketplace.

CHAPTER 13

Managing Our Money

Most of us blissfully enjoy many of the good things in life without ever needing to know how they work or how they are made. Take cars, for instance. We fill them up with gas, change the oil regularly, check the tires, and we're good. What about the internet? We plug this cable into that outlet, hit the power button, and leave the discussions on gigabytes and coding to the experts, right? And while we might love hot dogs, we might be better off not knowing how they're actually made.

The same often is true for an organization's finances—even for faculty and staff in a college of business. For a few, finances are their life's work. They've written papers, articles, and books on it. They research it, teach it, and help create the next-generation versions of it. For many, however, it's not a topic of concern during their daily routines.

I confess I didn't give much thought to what was under the hood of our college's financial engine. Now I realize it's not only essential to my role as dean of the Walton College, but something every member of our team needs to understand. Very few faculty or staff members need to understand finances the way a mechanic understands an automobile's engine or the way a computer programmer understands coding. But they all need to understand where the money comes from, how it's allocated in the college, and why it matters.

My deeper education into the college's financial processes and policies began in 2007 when I became the holder of the Garrison Endowed Chair in supply chain management. It was personally important, not to mention an expectation of others, that I steward those resources wisely.

When I became Chair of the Department of Supply Chain Management in 2011, I learned a great deal about our finances and accounting processes from David Hyatt. He was my assistant department chair, but he also was the former CFO of the Walton College and one of the architects of the integrated business, financial, and HR system we used for many years.

My education continued in 2013 when I was named as an SEC Academic Leadership Fellow. We studied the financial processes and procedures of a university by comparing ours to similar processes and policies at the University of Tennessee and the University of Florida.

That background helped prepare me for my role as dean, but not because I had become an expert. Quite the opposite. As with so many things in life, the more I learned, the more I realized how much I still needed to know. So, when I agreed to serve as interim dean in April 2015, it occurred to me that I really needed to get an even more detailed handle on the financials of the college and the financial processes, policies, and procedures of both the college and the university.

The office of the dean delegates the responsibility of the Walton College's finances and accounting to our CFO and our Accounting Center, but that doesn't mean I could abdicate this responsibility.

If you reflect back to my framework, it's easy to see why. Leadership is about coping with change, so a leader sets direction, aligns people to a shared vision, and motivates and inspires. And a leader needs the skills of sensemaking, relating, visioning, and inventing. Our vision and direction are tied to the financing that supports them, and I can't align, motivate, or inspire others if I don't understand our budget and financial processes. I can relate to the challenges our faculty and staff face, but I can't do much to solve their problems if I don't understand our finances. And I certainly can't make sense of our finances for others or come up with inventive solutions and approaches if I don't understand how these things work and why they matter.

All of this comes into play with every constituent group imaginable—faculty and staff within the college, students, university administrators, and, of course, donors and alumni. Thus, to avoid the trap of delegation with abdication, I had no choice but to dig in deeply. It was the only way I could effectively and accurately talk shop with the CFO of the Walton College and the CFO of the university, and it was the only way I could lead effectively in accordance with my framework. There was no reasonable shortcut.

The day after I signed on the dotted line and became interim dean, I set up an appointment with our former CFO and Tanya Russell (then the director of the Accounting Center and now our CFO). Tanya was, and continues to be, extremely patient with me and my unending stream of questions and concerns.

I also quickly met with Tim O'Donnell, the CFO of the university and vice chancellor for Finance and Administration, and Kathy Van Laningham, the vice provost for planning. Before joining the University of Arkansas in 2013, Tim had a twenty-two-year career with Southwestern Energy, where he led the company's finance and treasury, so we were very fortunate to have someone of his caliber at our university. We now have Chris McCoy as CFO. He was formerly CIO of the University of Arkansas, and he is a very strategic thinker and a highly competent leader.

Kathy managed the university's personnel budget, among many other responsibilities, and she is a tremendous source of institutional knowledge. She and the provost are the key people I work with when we are trying to get new faculty positions or hire for replacements. Colleen Briney is now the vice provost for planning, and she has an extensive background in accounting and finance.

As I began the process of learning from these and other experts, I started doing some of my own financial modeling, which caused me to ask lots of questions and test my understanding. One thing I discovered was that misconceptions can stem from the names of the line items on some of our financial reports. Our annual Net Operating Revenue report, for example, includes a "Tuition" line item. In my mind, I imagined this represented the tuition generated by the Walton College. I was wrong. It actually represented a very narrow set of sources of tuition. Other sources showed up in other line items. That same report has a "state budget" line item. I figured this represented money that was allocated from the State of Arkansas to the University of Arkansas and then to the Walton College. That was partially correct. Other money is mixed into this, including some tuition.

The more I learned, the more comfortable I was with our financial reports, processes, procedures, and policies, but I was not comfortable with their clarity. So, I made it a priority to have consistent, regular, and easy-to-understand communication about these matters.

Clarity—in the terms used in our financial reports and in everything else involving our finances—promotes a stronger alignment on decisions and direction. With greater visibility and understanding, for instance, everyone is more aware of the constraints and tradeoffs we face as a college.

I began spreading this message throughout our college during a belt-tightening time in our history. Beginning in 2017, all colleges on campus were required to cut 1 percent from their budgets per year for the next three years. Each year, we needed to show the chancellor, provost, and CFO where we had cut and where we were reallocating funds in accord with the eight key priorities of the university that had emanated from our campus planning process.

This was a brilliant strategy by our chancellor because it helped ensure we were using our resources effectively and that the resources were advancing each unit of the university in the same direction—toward our campus-wide priorities. By regularly sharing about the priorities and the related financial constraints and tradeoffs, our faculty and staff were better aligned on the vision and direction and, therefore, better able to cope with the changes in effective ways. It was very challenging for us because we were growing so quickly.

Understanding our finances also was particularly important in 2020 when we had to make drastic adjustments on the fly because of the COVID-19 crisis. The state, for instance, reduced appropriations to the university by $8.2 million that year, and there was a great deal of uncertainty about our revenue streams and cuts we would need to make as we moved forward.

One key decision we made early on was to use one-time funding sources first to protect salaries and positions. We believed our finances would improve, so we didn't want to make short-term decisions that hurt employees. We needed to be looking at least two years out.

I spent a great deal of time during that period meeting with the provost, the vice chancellor of administration and finance, and the other deans, and in April 2020 we issued a joint statement to faculty and staff across the university outlining the core principles that would guide our budgeting decisions related to the crisis:

1. We will do all we can to ensure job and salary security, and will prioritize people over projects or building initiatives;
2. We will first suggest contingency cuts that use one-time only funds, meaning that any proposed cuts would hopefully be temporary and non-recurring;
3. We will do all we can to avoid permanent cuts to assure our greatest future success as a university;

4. We will be transparent in our units and across campus, letting you
   know the realities we may face as soon as we do;
5. We will help one another out—financially and otherwise—pooling
   resources even across units, when possible and allowed;
6. We will work to preserve revenue generating programs and delay
   non-essential hires as needed;
7. We will work together and dismiss any notion of only protecting
   our unit's interests—the university only does well if we all do well
   together;
8. We are and will work closely with the central administration to craft
   budget changes that minimize the impact of the reductions and
   maintain a strong university;
9. And, we will be right here with you, to help in any way we can.

Following the Money

Even though every university and college functions differently, there are
some common elements among most of them. Taking a look at how we
operate financially at the Walton College should at least provide a baseline
for any dean or would-be dean. Even if you lead in a nonacademic setting,
the example is helpful in understanding structure and identifying revenue
sources.

When I began sharing with faculty and staff about the finances of the
college, I started by giving them an overview of where the money comes
from, where it goes, and the structure we use to manage it. The easiest part
was explaining where the money goes, because about 80 percent of our
operating revenues are for salaries, wages, and fringe benefits. Most of the
remainder goes to maintenance (18 percent), which covers a wide array of
non-payroll expenses—everything from travel to subscriptions and memberships, supplies, databases, and registration fees.

Revenues, on the other hand, are much more diverse and, at times,
confusing.

Roughly 95 percent of the revenues that support the Walton College
come from six sources—the university allocation, endowments, special
program tuition, differential tuition, donations, and Teaching Equipment
and Laboratory Enhancement (TELE) fees. The college also receives
funding from grants, interest income, and other program revenue, which

includes room rentals, executive education, and conference registration revenue, but those combine to account for less than 5 percent of our budget.

The largest source of revenue for the Walton College is the university allocation. The University of Arkansas draws its revenue from state appropriations, tuition, fees, and other sources.

For instance, state appropriations were $116.5 million, and tuition and fees were $314.87 million for fiscal year 2021.[16] The university allocates part of that $431.37 million to the various units on campus, including the Walton College of Business. This allocation is often referred to as "state budget," but I consider it our "university allocation" because it isn't just state appropriations; it also includes tuition.

In 2020, the university allocation was 40 percent of the Walton College's revenue. The percentage changes from year to year due to changes in other income, such as gifts or revenue from our executive MBA program. Our university allocation percentage increased each year from 2014 to 2016, when it was 44 percent. Increases also can result from new funding of faculty positions; however, the formula is more complex.

For years, the second-largest source of revenue came from endowment income. Now, however, it's typically from differential tuition, which is the extra amount the college charges above the university tuition. Differential tuition is based on a percentage of the university tuition, and it is common for colleges of business and engineering because these colleges are more expensive to operate than most other colleges. The supply and demand for business professors, for instance, results in much higher salaries for these faculty members than for most professors in a university (other than medical school professors). Salaries represent the preponderance of costs in higher education. On the other hand, even though the tuition is higher for business degrees, the return on investment is higher.

The Walton College gets 80 percent of the differential tuition on our courses, while the university gets 20 percent. We do not receive a fixed percentage of the other tuition revenue we generate (it is a more complicated formula). From 2014 to 2020, differential tuition to the college increased from $3 million to $11.6 million. Most of that increase was due to enrollment growth, and, therefore, credit hour production growth, but some of it was due to the increase in the differential tuition percentage.

---

16. https://budgetua.uark.edu/Budget.aspx

The next largest source of revenue usually comes from the executive MBA (EMBA) program, online courses, certificate programs, the professional master of information systems (PMIS) program, and other special programs. This is labeled "tuition/application fees" in our financial statements. It doesn't include tuition from the undergraduate program and others, so I refer to this revenue as "special program tuition." The Walton College generated about $6 million in special program tuition in 2020, including $2.5 million from the EMBA, $2.7 million from undergraduate online revenue, and $678,000 from PMIS.

The university allocation and differential tuition are considered "hard money" because those revenue streams are more stable than revenue from "soft money" sources such as endowments that are tied to the performance of the stock market. That's why the university prefers to fund nine-month salaries for tenured and tenure-track professors with hard money.

Endowments are based on a three-year rolling average and are invested conservatively, which helps minimize and postpone the impact of economic downturns. Still, we had a significant drop in income during the latest recession. Our income from endowments dropped from $5.17 million in 2008 to $4.46 million in 2012. Since 2012, we have seen a recovery in endowment income. For fiscal year 2020, we had $6.6 million in endowment income—a five-year increase of about $800,000.

We are fortunate to have the income from our endowments, but we have to be careful about how we spend it and how we depend on it. As you can see, our annual income from the endowment was about $700,000 less for 2012 than it was for 2008. Fortunately, other sources of revenue were increasing over that timeframe, but that doesn't always happen. It is not easy to come up with $700,000 to cover that level of loss. That's why we need a solid buffer each year: we can't spend all our income each year.

The fifth largest source of revenue to the Walton College is from gifts and donations, which is currently about 13 percent of our revenue. This source, however, also can swing widely from one year to the next. For instance, benefactors who are over a certain age have the option of giving a planned gift, which is an amount of money we receive upon their death. A member of my advisory board recently gave a planned gift of just under a million dollars. But it might be decades before the actual revenue accrues to the college. We have been receiving planned gifts for years, so we periodically receive significant amounts of money that actually were given decades ago.

Helping to secure donations and new endowments is a big part of a dean's job, so I'm going to devote the next chapter entirely to that aspect of finances.

The six-largest source of revenue to the college is from TELE fees, which is often referred to as "dedicated revenue" because it is a steady 5.4 percent of the budget. TELE, which stands for Teaching Equipment and Laboratory Enhancement, is one of the fees charged to students. The fee's purpose is to provide, maintain, and upgrade state-of-the-art teaching and lab equipment and to provide support to students to help them use this equipment. We have used our TELE fees to keep classroom technology updated, provide high-quality computer labs, and to pay the salaries of technology personnel who work directly to support these endeavors.

It is great that over the years the number of sources of revenue has increased. We see this trend continuing. Having a portfolio of sources of income allows us to have less volatility, which makes planning easier. Sharing this information with the faculty and staff helps them align on the plan and execute their parts of it with a positive attitude. It also better equips them to make realistic suggestions about how we can plan for and operate in the future.

Managing a Big Budget Business

Universities are big businesses, and the business college often is one of a university's biggest units. The FY 2020 budget of the Walton College was $56 million. This represents an increase of about $13 million over five years.

The Walton College operates with a budget that's similar to many mid-sized businesses. In fact, thirty-five of the top fifty companies on the 2018 Inc. 5000 list of fastest-growing private companies in America had annual revenues that were less than the Walton College. A small but highly qualified team makes sure we operate effectively, and it's important for our entire faculty and staff to know that team and how it functions.

I mentioned that Tanya Russell is our CFO, but that's not technically accurate. Her official title is assistant dean for finance and administration, but she functions very much like any corporate CFO. She and her team are vital to our success because they develop and execute effective processes for clearly communicating with the college about our financial position and performance, while also applying continuous improvement techniques to some of our existing accounting processes.

Tanya oversees the Accounting Center,[17] and she also is responsible for human resources, the conferencing hub, and facilities. When it comes to the financial accounting, budgeting, management, and reporting, Tanya supports the strategic, efficient, and effective use of the Walton College's fiscal resources and provides an accurate accounting of their deployment. This allows our leadership team to make strategic decisions with our limited resources in mind. I meet with Tanya in regularly scheduled weekly meetings, in ad hoc meetings, and through frequent emails and phone calls.

The Accounting Center is a one-stop shop for all financial transactions in the college. They help navigate the rules and regulations to facilitate the purchases necessary for all of us to do our jobs. Whether it is office supplies or a research database, they help process those transactions as efficiently as possible. Additionally, they provide reporting, budgeting, and projections so we can deploy our resources strategically, as well as plan for the future to ensure financial sustainability. They also complete required reports to the financial affairs office and other offices across campus, as well as external reporting (e.g., the AACSB Business School Questionnaire).

Angie Coleman, the director of accounting, functions as the college's controller. She is responsible for the daily operations of the Accounting Center and its staff. She oversees transaction processing, financial reporting, internal controls and policy guidance. She assists department chairs, unit directors, and chair holders concerning policies, procedures, balances, and expenditures. She also assists with preparation of the Walton College budget and financial forecasts.

Angie's team, among other things, reviews transactions, prepares reconciliations, processes travel claims, trains new employees on the travel process, manages our accounts payable, troubleshoots purchasing related issues, and prepares the Walton College financial reports. These reports combine data from the university and the foundation that manages the finances of gifts from donors, which allows us to have a

---

17. The Accounting Center is different from the Department of Accounting. The Accounting Center performs accounting functions for the Walton College, whereas the Department of Accounting is an academic department, involved in teaching, research and service.

complete picture of our finances so we can make better strategic and operational decisions.

This team is essential to the operational and strategic management of the Walton College. They demonstrate excellence, professionalism, innovation, and collegiality, supporting our EPIC values as a college. And because we have limited resources and must make tradeoffs and timing decisions, they are also critical to our success in moving toward our vision and accomplishing our mission.

CHAPTER 14

Funding Our Future

N
o discussion of finances at a university would be complete without a few words on fund-raising.

Gifts contribute about 10 percent of the annual revenue of the Walton College, not counting endowed gifts and in-kind gifts. The people and entities who make these donations impact our college in a variety of significant ways. While endowed gifts are not classified as operating revenue to the college, the interest they earn in investment portfolios generates revenue for the college.

Very few colleges operate without contributions from donors, and donors seldom contribute to a cause they don't believe in. If we successfully live out our mandate, then the college will make a transformational difference in the lives of our students, faculty, and community. Donors will see this as a valuable investment for the good of society, so they will give to help us in our efforts. Those donations, in turn, allow us to continue our success, while also innovating and finding new ways to succeed, which attracts more donors.

Donors, of course, are a key audience for communication from a dean. When I socialize our narrative, I'm often doing so with donors or potential donors so they can catch the vision of our college. I do that in individual and group settings. Those donors want to know about our structure, strategy, and priorities. They want to understand how we are financed and how we use our revenues as good stewards. They want to hear success stories, from me and through our marketing efforts. And they want to feel involved and appreciated.

Ultimately, our development efforts are my responsibility and, given its increasing importance to our college, I put significant time and effort into our fund-raising. But it can't just fall on my shoulders, so part of my communication to other audiences about finances includes discussions about our donors. I want our faculty, staff, and students to understand the role of these donations and to appreciate those who contribute to our work. And I want them to believe in our mission so strongly that they do what they can to help us raise money.

Some members of our faculty are significantly engaged with development efforts in the college. Barbara Lofton and Synetra Hughes of the Office of Diversity & Inclusion, for instance, helped raise $100,000 from Generations Bank for the Fleisher Scholars program. The more we are able to match experts with benefactors who have targeted interests, the more likely we are to secure gifts and investments from people to further the goals and initiatives of the college.

There is no requirement or expectation for faculty to be directly involved in development, but for faculty who are interested, we enthusiastically allow them to join our efforts. And those who aren't involved directly often contribute by sharing what they know about the college in positive ways with the people they encounter.

One of the ways I encourage this is by using my "Message from Matt" email to highlight recent donations. Many of our donors give to existing scholarships or initiatives with very little fanfare, but with great impact that shouldn't be taken for granted by our faculty and staff. In April 2019, for instance, I sent an email highlighting thirteen recent donations—seven of them for around $50,000 and the others ranging from $142,000 to $2.5 million.

Another way I do this is by explaining the strategic importance of our Office of Development and External Relations, which is critical to our fund-raising efforts. John Erck, the senior director of development and external relations for the Walton College, reports directly to me, but a dotted line connects him to Katy Nelson, the associate vice chancellor for university development. His office includes three main areas: (1) Development, (2) Communications (website, alumni magazine, public relations for the college, social media, and other communications), and (3) Constituent Relations (the Arkansas Business Hall of Fame, donor stewardship, and a number of special events).

Those areas are highly interconnected, because all of them have some focus on alumni, friends of the college, and benefactors. The development part of the organization is charged with visiting with those constituents, keeping them connected to the college, and ultimately soliciting them for gifts. Many of our donors serve on my Dean's Alumni Advisory Council and my Dean's Executive Advisory Board, which are managed by the constituent relations team.

The constituent relations team also creates the stewardship reports and manages the Arkansas Business Hall of Fame selection process and event. That event is the single biggest opportunity for the college to steward and cultivate a number of its best prospects. And the communications team manages all the communications for the college—a large portion of which is dedicated to the specific media that targets alumni, friends, and benefactors of the college. All three main functions work together closely to create a unified, outward message for the college.

In addition to helping raise funds specifically for the Walton College, we, as a college, help raise money for the entire university. These university-wide campaigns ultimately benefit the Walton College, either by directly providing us with revenue or by raising the overall quality and reputation of the university and thereby lifting our boat with the rising tide.

In 2001, for instance, the University of Arkansas launched the public phase of its Campaign for the Twenty-First Century, and by June 22, 2005 the university had surpassed its $1 billion goal in gifts and pledges. Campaign Arkansas, which began in 2012 and ended in 2020, exceeded its fund-raising goal of $1.25 billion, and the Walton College accounted for $250 million of those funds.

These efforts have a monumental impact on research at the university and at the Walton College. The Campaign for the Twenty-First Century, for instance, led to more than 130 new endowed faculty chairs and professorships, which allowed us to hire and retain outstanding researchers and teachers. It funded endowments for the library and the graduate school, both of which have contributed to improvements in the quality and quantity of research at the university. And it funded the Honors College and 1,738 scholarships and fellowships, which contributed to the research mission of the university by helping us attract and retain high-quality students from Arkansas and enabling these students to engage in life-changing programs such as study abroad.

Reflecting on the success of past campaigns—not just in dollars raised, but in the impact made—has encouraged me and our team as we move into new efforts such as our current Campaign Arkansas initiative.

Confession

When it comes to my role in fund-raising, I need to make a confession: This was a major area of fear for me when I took the job as dean. In fact, it was one of the reasons I almost didn't take the job. I was afraid I couldn't do it.

Managing philanthropy is one of the toughest aspects of being a dean of a major business school. Most deans, and not just business school deans, feel intense pressure around philanthropy. It's a very measurable aspect of the job—either we hit our goals or we don't—so it's somewhat like being the coach of a major sports team. If you don't hit your numbers, your days will be numbered.

Coaches, however, are measured on wins and losses, and they are trained to coach for wins. Deans are measured (in part) on how well they raise funds for their college, but that's typically not an area of expertise for an incoming dean. In fact, the AACSB's 2017–18 Dean's Survey found that deans rank fundraising as one of the top two tasks they are "least prepared" to handle (along with accreditation management).

Like many academics, I consider myself a researcher and writer. I was trained to do research and write academic articles. I did that in graduate school, I did that as a professor, and that's what made me successful. When I became dean, all of a sudden I had to raise millions of dollars each year, and the very idea of this responsibility made me uncomfortable on many different levels.

One, I didn't think I had the skills I needed. Two, I didn't think it fit my personality. I'm relational and friendly, and I'm comfortable speaking to groups. But, truth be known, I'd rather be at home with my family than out raising money, even when I'm passionate about the cause. That's just the way I'm wired.

Just having a conversation about giving was unsettling. It sounds simple enough: *Have you ever thought about giving a scholarship in your name? Well, the chancellor has this Advance Arkansas Scholarship. And he'll match the payout of any endowment you create. For example, if you were to give $100,000 for an endowment that generates $4,000 per year, he will match that, so it will be $8,000 a year.*

Easy, right? But I had never done anything like that before.

When I ran my software company, I asked for money, but I was providing something in return for that money. If you wanted my software and you want my consulting services, you paid me for it. That seemed different than saying, *Would you give us $100,000 to fund a scholarship?*

As dean of the Walton College, I figured I would have to ask some form of that question over and over. For instance, in 2019–20 I expected to make between sixty and seventy-five development calls with a goal of yielding nine to twelve major proposals. To hit my goals, those proposals would need to land the Walton College an average of almost $3 million each. My goals were lower in my first year as dean, but they were still really big, at least in my eyes, and the thought of raising millions upon millions of dollars was a bit overwhelming. Failure felt inevitable, even for an eternal optimist like me.

I hit my goals that first year, but I thought I had picked all the low-hanging fruit and I still wasn't sure I was cut out for this part of the job. After hitting the goal each of the first four years, however, I realized this wasn't some impossible task. It was and is hard, and it still makes me uncomfortable from time to time, but I realized it just takes practice and the right attitude.

One thing I learned that made a huge difference was that I was wrong about how I looked at asking people for money. I thought there was a difference between asking for money for my consulting and software versus asking for money to fund a scholarship. There's really not.

In one case, they wanted my consulting because they wanted to solve a problem. They wanted value for their money. A scholarship is the same. If someone was born and raised in a poor part of Arkansas, they want to bless someone else from a poor part of Arkansas so they can get through school like they did and become successful like they did. Well, they're getting something. It's very esoteric, but it's real.

In my experience, people are not going to give huge amounts of money to anything unless they are getting some joy out of it. And it's not just the sheer joy of giving, it's joy from knowing that the gift is going to really make a difference in some tangible way. It's something they feel good about.

Professor of Philanthropy

When I made this attitude shift, conversations with donors and potential donors became much easier for me. But to really excel in this area of the job, I've found you still have to do two specific things really well. Fortunately, these two things are more aligned with my skills and experiences than I realized when I first took this job.

First, you have to know your school. Second, you have to know your donors.

Before you ever have a conversation about fundraising, you need to know everything there is to know about the college you lead. You need to know its strengths and weaknesses. You need to know what everyone is doing. You need to know numbers and you need to know stories. You need to know the history. You need to know the context. You need to know the "why" behind the activities.

What are we doing in finance? What are we doing in accounting? What are we doing in entrepreneurship? What are we doing in study abroad? How do we place students? How do we prepare students for the workforce? How do we recruit students? Where do we recruit students from? What percentage comes from Arkansas? Who are our top researchers? What are our professors publishing?

You have to know the people, the strategies, the tactics, the culture, the finances—everything. And you have to know it cold. You have to be able to get an A plus on the test about your school.

The better you know your school, the better prepared you are to respond to the questions and concerns donors have during the natural course of a conversation. When a donor describes the best thing she learned during her time as a student at Walton College and wants to know if you're still doing that, you are prepared to answer. Your answer might be yes, but most likely it's "We still do that, but not in the same way it was done when you were in school." Then you can share about what's new.

I have found that donors seldom get upset when you don't know something on the spot. If you don't know the answer and you can get it, that's fine. But if they are really passionate about something and you do know the answers, all of a sudden you can engage in a more meaningful conversation.

When it comes down to it, managing philanthropy is really all about building relationships and helping benefactors discover how to experience the joy of giving to the college. I believe if you do it properly, very little closing is necessary. Sometimes you don't even have to ask. You just have to show them how to do it from a practical perspective. You are talking about how they can help you and they're talking about how they can help you. All that's missing is the details around the *how*, which are seldom as simple as writing a check.

To have that conversation, you have to know your college. But you also have to know your donors. Before you meet with donors, you have to learn everything you can about them—their history with the college, details about their family, their passions related to their work, their passions outside of work, who their friends are, and, yes, even who their enemies are.

Navigating conversations with donors can be tricky, and, frankly, I'm not great at it. Our development team has to coach me. It's helpful to know, for instance, if Donor Jim and Donor Fred play golf on the weekends and take family vacations together every year in Aruba. It's even more helpful to know if they were in a business deal that went sour and they can't be in a room together. Here in Arkansas, a small state with a tight-knit business community, most leaders know each other and are friendly. But that's not always the case, not even within the same families.

Your study of donors doesn't just happen before you meet with them. It also takes place during the meetings. When you visit with your biggest donors, you have to listen and you have to ask questions and you have to take notes after, not during, the meeting.

I'll never forget one of the first meetings I had with a benefactor when I was a new dean. For starters, I am a morning person, and this meeting went from about 6 p.m. to 10:30 p.m. We also had a few glasses of wine during the visit, and I am a lightweight in that area. But I went back to my hotel room after the meeting, cleared my head, and spent about two hours making notes about our conversation.

Taking notes prepares you to follow up. You take what you learned and use it—not in some manipulative way, but to figure out how you, the college, and the donor can help each other. That might be with a financial donation, but it also might come in the form of advice. Donors and other business leaders have helped me as members of my advisory councils or just by providing insights during our conversations. These are highly successful people, and it's rare that they don't have ideas worth hearing and, in many cases, implementing. So I tell them what's going on, ask them what they think, and value their opinions.

Most of my meetings with donors don't have "ask for money" anywhere on the agenda. In fact, sometimes there is no agenda. For instance, I'm a football fan and I enjoy watching games, but I've never been one to attend tailgating parties. Now, I attend those parties before and sometimes after Arkansas Razorbacks football games. And while the Walton College has a suite at the stadium, I spend most of my time visiting with donors, those we invite or those who have their own suites. I see very little game action, but I learn a great deal about our donors and casually share as much as they want to know about what's going on at the Walton College.

Donors already know that you, as the dean, would love for them to make a financial contribution to the college. In fact, they typically won't meet with you if they aren't open to giving. How much they might give varies, but they come to the conversation with the desire to help. All you have to do is be prepared to create a path for them to help.

This takes work, but it's the work of a researcher. So as an academic, I was prepared for philanthropy. The only difference was that my field of study had shifted.

My big ah-ha moment was that this task is like any other. I have to do research, I have to think, I have to memorize, I have to take notes, I have to synthesize what I'm learning, and I have to write and speak about it. I realized the Walton College was my new subject. Just as I had become an expert in my academic discipline, now I needed to become an expert on the Walton College and I needed to become an expert on our biggest donors.

What's in a name?

When it comes to philanthropy, most of my time and attention, as you might expect, focuses on our wealthiest donors because the most efficient way for me to hit a multi-million-dollar goal is to get multi-million-dollar donations. John Erck and his team do most of the work when it comes to smaller donations. I'll support them when needed, and they help me in a multitude of ways when it comes to the bigger donations—which, by the way, also helps them meet their goals.

Because the donors I typically deal with are giving large amounts, I inevitably have to deal with the subject of naming rights. Interestingly, this isn't a particularly popular topic with deans or with donors. Deans aren't eager to bring it up, and donors aren't eager to talk about it.

I've found that most donors don't care if anyone knows about their gift; they would just as soon keep their giving anonymous. That was the case with Bill Dillard II when we began talking about what would become a $10 million donation to the Walton College accounting department. It was the case with Doug and Shelley McMillon when they donated $1 million to the university to launch an innovation studio. And it was the case with Clete Brewer and his family when they made a large donation to fund an entrepreneurship hub. They all told me they didn't need any recognition. They just wanted to help.

The same is true with many other donors, but naming rights are a valuable part of what makes a college successful. In fact, sometimes the name attached to the gift is just as valuable, if not more valuable, than the actual money. It helps more than most donors know that we have the William Dillard Department of Accounting, the McMillon Innovation Studio, and the Brewer Family Entrepreneurship Hub rather than some generic name for those initiatives. Those names tell students, alumni, employers, and the general community that someone successful thought enough of what we're doing to help fund our efforts.

The best example of this happened several years before I became dean. The Walton Family Charitable Support Foundation's $50 million donation to the college in 1998 was the largest gift at that time ever given to a public business school, but there was no quid pro quo. The family didn't require that we rename the college. In fact, Doyle Williams, the dean at that time the gift was made, had to talk them into it.

Now, I want to be clear on this: a $50 million endowment would have gone a long way toward improving what we do even if we were still known as the University of Arkansas College of Business Administration. But like the financial donation, the bang the college has gotten from the new name also is immeasurable and ongoing, and here's why: Most of the top fifty business colleges in the United States are named for a benefactor, but few of those benefactors are as widely known as Sam Walton. They might have been well-known in a city or state, but not so much nationally or globally. In fact, I would guess that most people would only recognize two of the names attached to those colleges—Kellogg (Northwestern's business college) and Marriott (Brigham Young's business college)—and that's because those also are current, strong corporate brands.

Sam Walton, of course, gives our college a widely recognized name, especially among people with an interest in business. The Walton name not only connects the business college to the biggest company ever created, but to the various disciplines that made Walmart such a successful enterprise— excellence in supply chain management, retail, entrepreneurship, global business, and so on.

Having the Walton name attached to the college honors Mr. Sam (as he was known) and his family, but it also genuinely helps the college. It gives us credibility and recognition, it encourages students to enroll in the college, it inspires other benefactors to support our efforts, and it motivates us to live up to the high standards represented by the Walton family legacy.

The Sam Waltons of the world, of course, are few and far between. We're fortunate, though, to have quite a few high-profile business leaders as donors. Attaching their names to buildings, centers, scholarships, and even departments gives a significant boost to the work we're doing with the donations that make it possible.

Gifts of this magnitude typically are years in the making. For instance, I had served as dean, counting my interim tenure, for a little less than a year when I first began a real relationship with Bill Dillard II. I knew who he was long before that, of course, and we had met a few times, but the relationship changed when I became dean. Our first lengthy meeting, was in April 2016 when John Erck and I spent about ninety minutes with Bill as he discussed his desire to increase a donation he had made to endow the corporate finance chair.

In a meeting a few months later with Bill and his brother, Alex, Bill asked about our greatest needs, and we had a good discussion about the challenge of keeping talent in the competitive accounting market. Bill, who earned his degree in accounting from the UA, asked to meet Gary Peters, who had taken over as chair of the accounting department. So Bill, Gary, John, and I got together that November. That's when we brought up the idea of a departmental naming gift. Bill was interested but made no commitment.

The next year, we continued to meet and Bill began contributing to a fund to endow the department. That September, Gary and Bill met on campus and Gary was able to share some of the details about the history of the department and what it would take to improve its reputation nationally. Bill was extremely interested in the types of students who chose accounting as a major and in the potential impact his gift could make.

At one memorable meeting, Bill invited a few of us to join him on one of his regular store tours. It was amazing how efficiently he moved through the store and how many details he knew about the store and its operations.

By November 2018, Bill had given around $5 million to the endowment fund, and by October 2019 he committed to get it to $10 million. He also agreed to name it in some way for his father or his family. That December, we settled on naming it for his father, the founder of Dillard's and also a graduate of the UA with a degree in accounting. Then in February 2020, almost four full years after our first meeting, we made a public announcement.

What's interesting is that I never thought of it as spending four years "working" to get a sizable donation. I thought of it as four years (and counting) of building a relationship with someone who loves his university and wants to help make it better. Bill really felt like the education he got from the University of Arkansas directly contributed to his success in business, and he is passionate about the value of an accounting degree.

"Most things in business involve understanding the numbers," he told me during a 2019 podcast interview. "I just don't see how you would expect to make intelligent business decisions if you don't have a good feel for numbers. . . . I just don't see how you do well in the world of business without an accounting background" (Waller 2019).

He has specific stories that illustrate how that's true, he told me, and he wanted to say "thank you" to his alma mater in a big way. Adding his family's name to the department not only allowed us to thank him, but it increases the value of his gift by adding value to the department's brand.

CHAPTER 15

Delivering Appreciation

Review the recent research on the value of showing appreciation to employees, and you will notice two very different takes on the workplace reality.

In 2018, Reward Gateway, a London-based employee engagement company, commissioned a study that produced results consistent with many similar surveys. The researchers surveyed 1,500 workers and 750 employers who were equally split from the UK, the US, and Australia. They found that 84 percent of "senior decision-makers" believed their company was doing enough to recognize "employees who demonstrate the values that their company cares most about." Meanwhile, 33 percent of employees said their employer didn't recognize them when they demonstrated the company's values (Reward Gateway 2018).

There's obviously a huge gap between the way leaders and employees see the same reality when it comes to recognition. That gap helps account for consistently poor employee engagement scores, which also are indicative of low productivity and/or high turnover.

On the other hand, studies like the one commissioned by Reward Gateway find a direct correlation between employees who feel recognized and companies that get high net promoter scores from their employees—in other words, employees who feel recognized are more likely to say they would recommend the company to friends and peers as a place to work. So it's imperative that leaders get this right—that they truly appreciate and recognize their employees for their good work and for living out the organization's values.

While recognition is vital to the success of any organization, it's especially critical when a wide variety of constituents play a role in the organization's success—you know, like a university. The Walton College, like any unit within a university, succeeds only when it is supported by the members of its faculty and staff, so part of my job is to make sure they know their hard work hasn't gone unnoticed. But a dean also must regularly recognize the achievements of students, the university's administrators, community and business leaders, alumni, and donors (who often fit in multiple categories). In other words, everyone who contributes to the success of the college should be encouraged and recognized by the dean; that's one of the ways a leader motivates and inspires.

Recognition also is a means for providing information to stakeholders about what's going on and what success looks like, so it's a way of reinforcing the direction you've set as a leader and aligning those stakeholders to a shared vision.

Recognition is an important part of our marketing efforts because it's one of the ways we genuinely share how our values are lived out and provide something of value to others. The reality is, we do care about the desires and feelings of our constituents. We are proud of their achievements, so we want to tell the world about them.

Personally, I find joy in recognizing the achievements of others. When I learn about their accomplishments, my enthusiasm is not feigned, and it makes me want to tell others about their successes. I believe this attitude has given me an advantage in life. I think others can sense my joy in their achievements, and that strengthens our relationship.

Thoughtful Reflection

My commitment to recognition as dean of the Walton College begins with a commitment to thoughtful reflection.

I noted earlier that I've committed our mandate to memory, which allows me to regularly reflect on our mission, vision, and values. And, of course, I spend a good deal of time reflecting on our current and future issues—where we are and where we're going. Whether I am working out in the morning or driving across the state to an event, I'm always looking for time to reflect on what's happening that impacts the college. Inevitably, that reflection allows me to identify the people and groups who are executing at a high level to make us all successful. This produces an immense sense of gratitude within me, and that gratitude fuels my desire to find thoughtful ways to recognize those people for whom I'm so grateful.

Thoughtfulness, as author Mark Sanborn notes, adds a deeper meaning to ordinary recognition and appreciation.

"Thoughtful people are those who pay attention to the people around them, reflect on the situation, and then choose to react and act in a purposeful and loving way," he says. "It takes a bit more consideration and time than simply being nice" (Sanborn 2018).

Recognition is an assignment I own as the dean of the Walton College. I suspect many leaders are less successful than they think when it comes to recognizing employees because they have assigned it as a task to someone else or created a program that's supposed to check that particular box.

We're great at employee recognition, they say. *We name an Employee of the Month, we have a company picnic, and we send out a press release whenever someone wins an award. How could they not feel recognized and appreciated?*

Recognition and appreciation, however, aren't events; they are a process. And it's not a process a leader assigns, it's a process a leader models. Everyone takes part in it, but in collaboration, so that it becomes a natural tenet of the culture.

When done well, appreciation and recognition take place organically, as well as proactively.

Organic recognition involves ordinary interactions. It can be as simple as saying two words: "Thank you." For those words to have an impact, however, they have to be genuine, which means you need a legitimate reason for saying them. That comes from thoughtful reflection.

One of the ways to make this happen is to start each day by thinking through your schedule. If you know you have a meeting with the team that produces your website, for instance, you can reflect on their accomplishments and the things each of them does well. Then you can thank them during the meeting in very specific, heartfelt ways. You also want to go into every meeting with an openness to seeing something worth recognizing. If you're looking for it, you almost always will find it.

Organic recognition can occur in one-on-one conversations or during meetings with small groups. It can even occur when the person you are recognizing isn't there. In fact, one of the most powerful ways to show appreciation for someone is to do it when they *aren't* around. Word almost always gets back to them, and, when it does, they can't help but feel honored.

Proactive recognition involves making gratitude part of my routine. I try never to leave a meeting without recognizing the people involved for the work they've done, regardless of whether I'm meeting with faculty and staff, students, administrators, or alumni and donors. And just about every email I send includes some element of gratitude.

Furthermore, proactive recognition involves a commitment to formal programs, policies, and best practices, all of which have greater impact when they are not only supported by but practiced by me as dean. We generate a ton of press releases recognizing our staff, faculty, students, and alumni, for instance. And we promote that type of recognition on social media, with stories, photos, and videos on our websites and in print publications, and with signage throughout our hallways. The Walton College has a fantastic communications department that shares our success stories with the world. As dean, I'm also deeply involved—sharing gratitude for others through mass emails to faculty, staff, and students; through podcasts and videos; during meetings and speeches; and through posts on a variety of social media platforms.

Shining an Intentional Light

I went through a few years' worth of emails I've sent out to intentionally recognize a person or group and realized most of them fit into at least one of seven buckets: student accomplishments, promotions and new hires, faculty and staff accomplishments, values in action, departments that excel, alumni achievements, and general gratitude.

Here's what those look like.

Student accomplishments. When I brag on the accomplishments of students, I always try to put that praise in the right context by providing details about those achievements.

For instance, I wouldn't just send a note acknowledging that two of our accounting students were in the top seventy-five performers in the US on the CPA exam. I also would point out that more than ninety-three thousand people took the exam that year, which meant we had two students in the top 0.08 percent. And when our portfolio management classes formed a combined team that took first place in the Graduate Value Portfolio category of a NASDAQ-sponsored finance competition in New York, I pointed out that the event included more than 1,400 participants from 147 universities in thirty-seven countries.

Another great example of this involves our Office of Entrepreneurship and Innovation, which has been recognized in *The New York Times, CNN Money,* NPR, *Inventors Digest,* and the *NASDAQ* because of its students' achievements. Every year, and sometimes multiple times during the year,

I'm able to sing the praises of these students, especially when it comes to their successes in start-up competitions. Our students have won twenty-seven national business plan competitions, which is more than any other university. They also have won more than $3 million in prize money since 2002 and raised more than $60 million to build their businesses.

Every time our students win an award, finish strong in a competition, or otherwise represent the college well, it's an opportunity to celebrate them for their hard work and the EPIC value of Excellence. It's also an opportunity to recognize the faculty and staff who have taught them, coached them, encouraged them, and led them—everyone who played a role in helping the students succeed.

Four of our students, for instance, once took fourth place at a business case study competition at the Kelley School of Business. There were thirty-eight schools at the event, and our students beat teams from such notable universities as Yale, Ohio State, Penn State, Michigan, Tennessee, Texas, Arizona, and Cal-Berkeley. It provided an opportunity to recognize the students, but also the Office of Diversity and Inclusion (which the students were representing in the competition), while noting how these efforts supported our values.

Here's another example: After our 2016 commencement ceremony, I sent out a one-paragraph email commending one of our students, Brittany Brunson, for delivering a memorable and poetic speech. And, with her permission, I attached a copy of the speech for everyone to read. This not only was a way of recognizing Brittany, but everyone who had played a role in her education and personal growth during her time at Walton College.

Promotions and new hires. Because the Walton College is growing, we often find ourselves hiring new people to new positions and promoting those who have helped us achieve success. These are obvious opportunities to express gratitude and recognize our employees for their great work.

I often mention new hires and promotions in my regular emails and social media posts, and sometimes I find opportunities to feature these employees in a podcast or video. Not only that, each fall, I host a new-faculty event at my home. This is an opportunity for them to get to know each other; meet key administrators; hear me talk about our culture, mission, vision, and values; and experience our culture firsthand.

In addition to recognizing our new hires, I like to acknowledge the people who helped hire them. In many cases, we form search committees to find just the right person for a position. So I think it's important to recognize those committee members by name for the work they put into helping us build a quality team.

Faculty and staff accomplishments. Each Spring we present faculty with seven formal awards—All Around, Teaching, Research, Service, Diversity, Adjunct Teaching, and Graduate Teaching. These awards recognize faculty members for their work and give me an opportunity to connect their accomplishments to our mission, vision, and values.

Throughout the year, opportunities to recognize faculty and staff abound. They are honored by peer groups, they lead successful initiatives, they are selected for fellowships, and, of course, they do ground-breaking research.

Because research is such an important component of our mission, it's critical that I celebrate our successes in that area. I pay close attention to rankings that show how frequently our faculty is published and how often their work is cited. For instance, the University of Arizona ranks information systems researchers by the h-index. In early 2019, I noticed that four of our professors—Varun Grover, Mary Lacity, Viswanath Venkatesh, Rajiv Sabherwal—were ranked in the top 4 percent, so I mentioned that in my weekly "Message from Matt" email.

I share tools like ResearchGate, Google Scholars, and Digital Measures so that faculty can follow these metrics on their own, but I also sum up the findings.

At least once a year, I send an email to the college that emphasizes the strategic importance of research to the Walton College. This not only reinforces that part of our mission, but allows me to use examples in ways that celebrate our team's successes. For instance, in late 2017 I was able to point out that we had published 542 articles in scholarly journals, earned 127 "best paper" recognitions, and seen our research cited more than 15,000 times.

Another chance to honor our employees is by recognizing the contributions of leaders when they change or add to their roles. In August 2020, for instance, Jeff Hood, Barbara Lofton, and Mike Waldie all were promoted to the role of assistant dean. This gave me an opportunity to send an email sharing some of the highlights of their accomplishments as leaders throughout the years.

I even recognize some employees who are leaving for other jobs. We hate to lose great people, but that's a natural byproduct of our success. If we're doing our jobs well, we will prepare people for new challenges—within the Walton College or elsewhere. They might leave for another university, for a corporate job, to start a company, to lead a nonprofit, or to spend more time with family. Regardless, their contributions to the college are worth celebrating—not just to pat them on the back, but to acknowledge the impact our team had on that individual's journey.

Rachel Burton, for instance, worked in development roles at the Walton College for more than ten years, then became director of a nonprofit serving adults with developmental disabilities. A note she allowed me to share with the college was a testament to our culture:

> It's the experience I have gained here that has given me the courage to take on this new challenge. I'll be channeling each of you daily and applying everything I have learned from working with you all. I don't intend to give up the friends I've made here and I know that our incredible network of like-minded professionals will make me an even greater asset to the mission of Life Styles. Thank you and please keep in touch!

Values in action. Every time someone exemplifies our values, I see it as an opportunity to celebrate and offer recognition.

In 2019, for instance, marketing professor Dinesh Gauri worked with the *Journal of Retailing* to organize the Retailing Thought Leadership Conference, which drew more than 150 attendees from thirty universities and more than thirty companies. The event contributed to our vision of thought leadership and our mission of advancing and disseminating business knowledge in retail. One way I let Gauri know his efforts were valued was by sharing that story in an email to the executive committee and copying Gauri.

Sometimes acknowledgments are quite formal. In addition to the annual faculty and staff awards, which are chosen by committees, I created the Dean's EPIC awards to spontaneously recognize someone who exemplifies our values in some outstanding way. I select the winners and hand out the awards whenever someone deserves to get one. I give out an EPIC Award for overall commitment to the values, but I also give out awards specific to Excellence, Professionalism, Innovation, and Collegiality.

When I choose someone for an award, I set up an appointment with them in my office and surprise them with a certificate and some words of encouragement. We take a photo, which I email to the executive committee. Then we recognize the winners in a faculty/staff meeting.

One EPIC Award went to Kim Petrone, an accomplished attorney who joined our faculty in 2014 as an instructor. In 2019, she became the coordinator for our business law class, which is a required course for all of our business students. Around 1,300 freshmen take the course each year. When Kim took on the new role, she led a meeting that resulted in several proactive strategies for helping support our student success initiatives. Among other things, she coordinated with the Math Department on scheduling exams so that students wouldn't face a final in business law, finite math, and algebra in close proximity. She also came up with a plan to give students an opportunity to recover if they performed poorly on their first test.

Her efforts reflected a commitment to continuous improvement in areas that are part of our overall strategic plan. She demonstrated Excellence, Professionalism, Innovation, and Collegiality in her leadership, and she encouraged others to adopt a similar mindset.

I also try to recognize our faculty and staff when they go above and beyond on special projects or with acts of service.

When the university held an "All in ror Arkansas" birthday fundraiser, I was overwhelmed by the support we got from our faculty and staff. So, I sent out a special email praising those efforts, and specifically recognizing several people. Anne O'Leary-Kelley, a professor and senior associate dean, had given the gift that put the university over its original "100K in a Day" goal, allowing for a new push goal. And Jeff Hood, Autumn Parker, and Molly Rapert generated a ton of interest in the event on social media. Calling them out specially and everyone in general was one way to recognize that fund-raising is a vital role we all play in the health of the college.

I also send out a special thank-you note following the annual Walton College Block Party. This is an important event, because it allows our students to meet and get to know our faculty and staff. It is only successful because more than forty faculty and staff members volunteer to be there and truly engage with the students. It is a wonderful picture of how we can live out our EPIC values, so I point that out in an email and often list the names of all the faculty and staff members who participated. And the next year when we are planning the event, I can reference those volunteers again to help encourage them and additional volunteers to take part.

In 2020, I was particularly aware of the need to recognize those who put our values into action, because the pandemic brought challenges and stress unlike anything we'd ever seen. I was particularly proud of my executive team for how they led over that summer and into the fall as we returned to limited face-to-face instruction. Here's an example of an email I sent them:

I commend each of you for successfully preparing us for the students' return to campus.

Yesterday I walked through all three buildings three times, talking with many students, staff and faculty. I queried each of them carefully about how things were going. Everything was working more smoothly than I could have expected and I'm convinced it is because of each of you and your team. You are a high-performance team. I've worked with many teams in my career, and this is one of the most impressive in terms of what you all have achieved in an environment of high uncertainty and high equivocality. I know there were some problems yesterday, but I think it went much better than it would have without this team. Your success benefits the students, faculty, staff and the entire university. Thank you!

#RazorbacksTogether
BE HAPPY. BE SAFE. BE EPIC.
Best regards,
Matt

I sent a similar email to the executive committee and the leaders of our executive MBA program after visiting those classes the first week we returned to class. I commented on how well students were adhering to social distancing and mask guidelines, while staying engaged in lectures and group discussions. It also gave me an opportunity to state my appreciation for the high quality of lectures given by faculty members Chris Hofer, Jeff Murray, John Aloysius, and Vikas Anand.

Departments that excel. Sometimes the purpose of proactive recognition is to help prevent people from slipping into a silo mentality where all they think about is their particular part in the organization. In a research university setting, it's easy for faculty to get lost in their work and lose sight of the bigger picture and how everyone works together to make the whole greater than the sum of its parts. So once a year I usually send out an email that thanks every unit in the college for its contribution of providing high quality business education to our students.

Again, this is an opportunity to re-state things like our values, mission, vision, and strategic initiatives. But I also include a one- or two- sentence praise for every unit that's very specific to the role that unit plays. In 2016, for instance, that email included twenty-four paragraphs of praise, because there were twenty-four units represented in the Walton College. I wanted the people within each unit to realize I didn't take their good work for granted, and I also wanted them to see how the contributions of other units were part of our collective success.

I also look for opportunities to highlight the achievements of different offices and departments throughout the year. For instance, in 2016 I sent an email noting that our Department of Accounting was making significant progress in climbing the research rankings—from No. 34 to No. 26 worldwide in overall research, to No. 4 in archival audit research, to No. 2 in archival systems research, to No. 7 in PhD archival audit research, and to No. 1 in PhD accounting information systems research.

Finally, I seek opportunities to recognize departments and offices. Each February, in recognition of Black History Month, I typically send out an email recognizing the work done by our Office of Diversity and Inclusion. Other groups I've recognized for their work includes our clinical/teaching faculty, the Tyson Center for Faith and Spirituality in the Workplace, the Walton Conference Hub (which provides meeting space for events), human resources, and the Beta Gamma Sigma honor society.

Alumni contributions. In many ways, the success of our alumni is the strongest testimony to the quality of our work as educators. Our graduates have to go do the hard work that leads to success, and some have what it takes to succeed regardless of the quality of their formal education. But all of them will have a better chance at success if we've done our jobs well and taught them not only the theories of business but how to think for themselves and apply what they've learned in the context of their lives.

We honor them and each other by recognizing their achievements, and we do this in a number of ways. The most formal is the Arkansas Business Hall of Fame, which is housed in our Reynolds Center for Enterprise Development. The Walton College honors inductees with a banquet each year where we show a video highlighting their achievements, with promotional materials about their induction, and, of course, with their inclusion in the actual Hall. We also honor alumni during our annual awards banquet by presenting a lifetime achievement award, an entrepreneur of the year award, and an outstanding service award.

I personally work hard to recognize the inductees and award winners in my email, podcasts, social media, and video messages. I also intentionally recognize the team that runs the Hall of Fame, because they showcase our values of excellence and professionalism by helping us select and honor alumni who have lived those values.

Recognizing our alumni, of course, isn't limited to a few events during the year. One of the things I do consistently as dean is recognize alumni by highlighting their work in podcasts, blogs, articles, and video interviews. I often reference those who are members of my Dean's Alumni Advisory Council and my Dean's Executive Advisory Board for their contributions to the college.

One of the best opportunities to show appreciation for alumni is during Black History Month. This isn't the only month when we recognize alumni of color, but it provides a natural opening to praise their achievements.

When donors give to the Walton College, of course, there's a natural opportunity to express our gratitude in all number of ways—with press release, articles on our print and online publications, by attaching the donors name to some aspect of the program, and simply by looking for opportunities to point out how the funding is benefiting us whenever possible.

In fiscal year 2016, for instance, we raised more than $3 million in new scholarship money, some of it endowed and some not. One of my emails to faculty and staff that year made a point to recognize one of those donors— Carter Tolleson, a 2001 graduate of the Walton College who had done well financially after founding a wealth management company with his father. After meeting a few times with Carter, it became clear from his manner- isms, expressions, and words that he found true joy in giving to those in need who wanted to attend the Walton College. And because of his dona- tion, students who otherwise couldn't have continued their education were given an opportunity that changed their lives for the better. Connecting stories like Carter's to the students who benefit is a tangible way of sharing how we live out our mandate in powerful ways.

General gratitude. Jon Dorenbos played fifteen seasons in the National Football League, but he is perhaps best known as a magician who was a contestant on the television show *America's Got Talent*. He finished in third place on Season 11 of the show, then returned in 2019 and finished in the top twelve of *America's Got Talent: The Champions*.

I love his story, because it epitomizes not only the grit it takes to succeed in life but the value of appreciating the journey—even the most difficult parts. And Dorenbos had plenty of those. When he was twelve, his mother was killed and his father was convicted for committing the murder. His father went to prison, and Dorenbos went to a foster home. He was a good athlete in high school, but not heavily recruited in any sport. He was a linebacker and running back at a junior college when a friend suggested he transfer to the University of Texas El Paso and try out as a long snapper. He studied some videos on long-snapping, made the UTEP team, and later played in the NFL for the Buffalo Bills, Tennessee Titans, and Philadelphia Eagles. But his career ended after a routine physical revealed an aortic aneurysm that required open-heart surgery. That's when magic became his full-time job.

Here's what I think of most when I think of Jon Dorenbos: He ends each magic performance with the same line: "It's a great day to be alive."

That's the type of gratitude I hope others hear from me and see in me each day, and I never want to take for granted that others know I'm thankful. Like Dorenbos, I want them to hear it from me regularly.

When the "interim" tag was removed from my title, for instance, I sent out a specific thank-you email. I had felt a ton of support and encouragement during my time as interim dean, and I wanted the faculty and staff to know how much that meant to me. I also wanted them to know how thankful I was for what I had learned during the interview process, and how grateful I was to step into a situation with so many talented people who already were moving us in the right direction. This email, of course, allowed me to reinforce our values and our direction, so I not only was thanking people but aligning them and encouraging them as well.

The theologian John MacArthur once wrote, "Love is action, not abstraction" (MacArthur 2013). I feel the same way about gratitude. It's not a concept to ponder. It has to be a way of life.

The How-To's of Gratitude

One of the most important pieces of any recognition is the part that follows the word *for*. It's easy to stand at the front of a faculty and staff meeting and say something like, "Thank you all for the wonderful work you do." If you leave it at that, the cynics will likely snicker back with something like, "You have no idea what we actually do." That's a culture killer.

I confess I have a tendency to go a bit overboard when stressing the *for what* part of an appreciation message. For instance, my annual email during "Staff Appreciation Week" identifies twenty-six things our staff regular does that helps us succeed:

1. Thank you for advising our students.
2. Thank you for supporting our research.
3. Thank you for guarding our time so that we can conduct research.
4. Thank you for helping us collect data for our research.
5. Thank you for helping us organize and manage research seminars.
6. Thank you for helping us develop and distribute surveys.
7. Thank you for processing our travel.
8. Thank you for following up with us on tasks we need to complete.
9. Thank you for helping to retain our students.
10. Thank you for all of the administrative support provided for our educational processes.
11. Thank you for ensuring that we are improving our educational processes and achieving our educational goals.
12. Thank you for helping our students improve their written and oral communication skills.
13. Thank you for helping our students make career decisions.
14. Thank you for being kind to our students.
15. Thank you for helping our students prepare for interviews.
16. Thank you for helping our diverse students be included in our community.
17. Thank you for helping our students exemplify academic excellence, leadership, and civic duty to the community.
18. Thank you for helping our students find and secure scholarships.
19. Thank you for maintaining external relations with our constituencies.
20. Thank you for providing reliable and advanced technology for our students, faculty, and staff.
21. Thank you for providing the information we need.
22. Thank you for supporting our grant proposals.

23. Thank you for maintaining and coordinating our facilities.
24. Thank you for measuring, processing, controlling, and communicating our financial information.
25. Thank you for managing our meeting rooms, breakout rooms, boardrooms, auditorium and meal function areas.
26. Thank you for solving problems that arise.

Even with all of that, I knew I had left some things out, but hopefully they got the heart of my message: I was thankful for the specifics of their part in our success.

Recognition and My Framework

All of the communication that reflects recognition fits within my leadership framework. It helps me set direction, align people to a shared vision, and motivate and inspire. And it allows me to practice the capabilities of a leader by sensemaking, relating, visioning, and inventing. I may not use all of those capabilities or perform all of those roles every time I recognize someone or some group, but I try to think through them all and apply them as needed with every opportunity. And it's not unusual for several pieces of the framework to come into play.

This letter to faculty and staff that went out at the end of the Fall 2017 semester, for instance, speaks to direction, aligning on shared vision, and motivation and inspiration, and it exemplifies the use of sensemaking, relating, visioning, or inventing to communicate the message:

12/11/2017
Good Morning!
This has been an EPIC semester. I'm going to discuss a few of my observations that have caused me to label this semester as EPIC.

(Note: The first paragraph referenced our Be EPIC values, which reinforced our shared vision for living them out.)

This semester I have heard of or observed on several occasions faculty and staff demonstrating enthusiasm and concern for students. This is conducive to an EPIC educational environment and it inspires our students to do their best. It is encouraging to me personally and makes me proud of the faculty and staff of our College. Thank you!

Here we are in the midst of finals week and I'm still hearing of the remarkable achievements that so many of you have accomplished this semester. Most weeks of the semester I have students in my office and I ask them for feedback on the Walton College's performance. I ask them about their learning experiences in courses and about their experiences in dealing with the many service functions of the college. I know how much time and effort it takes to do an EPIC job in the classroom, in preparing for class, in grading assignments, in advising students, et cetera, so please know how grateful I am for what so many of you have done this semester. Our college has a promising future in business education as you continue to provide this outstanding level of service to our students. What you are doing is also a great service to our University and the State of Arkansas.

(Note: The next two paragraphs expressed my heartfelt gratitude, which was intended to encourage, motivate, and inspire. By referencing specifics, I reinforced those positive behaviors. By referencing my experiences with students and my experiences as an instructor, I was relating to the experiences of our faculty and staff. And by referencing my belief in our promising future, I was speaking to our direction and vision as a college.)

I am also aware of the tremendous research accomplishments this semester. Your persistence with the manuscript review processes of various refereed journals and your passion for various research topics has paid off. We are having lots of publication successes especially in terms of the quality of research and the journals where the research has been submitted or accepted. Well done. (You may remember from previous emails that we are creating metrics and processes to measure our research and discovery successes. In Digital Measures I can run a report on the college for "intellectual contributions," which includes papers that are under review, R & R, accepted or published. This morning I ran the report and reviewed the intellectual contributions from July 1 to date. I run this report periodically. I will run it again during the break and study it more thoroughly. Some faculty only enter research that has been accepted or published, while others include papers in the review process. I appreciate being able to see research in the review process, but either way is fine.) In addition to the metrics, I have learned of many anecdotes of successes this semester in terms of faculty achieving invitations to revise and resubmit manuscripts at top journals and in terms of interesting and relevant research findings. I'm always thrilled to learn of such achievements so please never be concerned that I might think you are bragging. It is my pleasure to share your joy of achievement.

(Note: The next paragraph, while a bit lengthy, served an important purpose, because research is so critical to our mandate. It is one of three functions, along with teaching and service, that are mentioned in our vision, and it is one of our strategic initiatives. I was able to encourage our faculty for their successes, while also applying sensemaking by giving them information about our new metrics and processes.)

In addition to having students in my office during most weeks of the semester, I also frequently have faculty in my office. For those of you who have been in my office, you know that I often ask about your research and teaching during the semester. I don't ask those questions from a judgmental perspective by any means, but I simply enjoy learning of your achievements and successes. Since June of 2015, I would say this semester tops them all in terms of the impressive achievements of faculty, staff, and students that I have learned of in a given semester.

I want to tell of my sincere gratitude on these achievements this semester. Without your leadership, dedication, expertise, and hard work, we would not have been able to make so much progress this semester as a college. Your individual contributions and team contributions toward our progress cannot be overstated.

This week we are in the "final" stretch of the semester. Thank you for all of the effort in grading finals, projects and various other assignments, and for calculating grades for all of the students. Some students will be pleased with their achievements and some will be disappointed. Thank you for rejoicing with the students who are pleased and for being compassionate with those who are disappointed. I believe this type of behavior is the norm for Walton College faculty and staff and I deeply appreciate it.

(Note: The next three paragraphs heaped more sincere praise on the faculty and staff for their fine work, while also setting direction and encouraging them for the stretch run to end the semester.)

Soup Day, provided by UGPO, is another reason for our EPIC semester. Dead Day Soup Day[18] is a tradition in the Walton College that brings together faculty and staff in an informal and fun atmosphere. Associates in UGPO and a few others bring soups in crockpots for lunch to celebrate the end of the semester. I really enjoy visiting with faculty and staff during this warm and enjoyable event. (My favorite soup was the butternut squash soup.) Thank you to the associates in UGPO for providing Soup Day once again and a special thank you to Autumn for organizing and planning Soup Day. It looked to me like we had a record turnout, which is one of the reasons we went through the soup so quickly. You might want to make a note to come early next year since we can go through the soup in no time.

The Walton College Mix and Mingle was also a great way to wind down our EPIC semester. Thank you to the Special Events Committee and Staff Council for planning and organizing the celebration and party. Thank you to Nidhi for leading this event and to Courtney for participating in the planning and organizing. The band played rock, country, and Christmas music. Thanks to Dub for paying for the band!

(Note: The next two paragraphs focused on service, which also is part of our vision statement. Again, I provided specifics, including thanks to several people by name, used the relating capability by making it clear I was there for the events, and motivated and inspired the faculty and staff to continue their efforts in service.)

Many of you use the time between semesters to work on research and prepare for the Spring Semester, but I hope each of you also take some time off to relax and enjoy time with friends and family.

---

18. Dead Day provides students with a day of no classes or other mandatory activities prior to the start of final exams each semester. The Dead Day Soup Day event is an optional activity for those who want a break from their studies—and some darn good soup.

This will be the last "Message from Matt" until sometime early next semester (although I might send an email under a different title if it becomes necessary).

Have a great week!

Best regards,

Matthew Waller

(Note: I ended by relating to the tendency of some on our faculty and staff to overwork during their break. I've felt that pull myself many times, but I know the importance of rest and wanted to encourage them to take the appropriate time off.)

No matter what your approach to recognition, I've found it most effective when it comes from the heart, when it speaks to specifics, and when it is both organically and proactively practiced. When it hits those buttons, the people you appreciate will truly feel appreciated, and they will continue to work with you to achieve success.

CHAPTER 16

A Balanced Life

The graduation ceremonies in May 2019 have come to represent a snapshot of my experience as the dean of a business school and the challenges that come with trying to balance my work with other interests, most notably, my family.

What made this graduation day unique was that Grant Waller, one of our four children, was donning a cap and gown and collecting his undergraduate diploma from the College of Engineering. Our family planned to be there for Grant's big event, of course, and John English, the dean of the College of Engineering at the time, agreed to let me sit on stage and hand my son his diploma.

This created a logistical challenge, however, because the graduation ceremony for the Walton College was the same day. In fact, the two ceremonies overlapped and were in different buildings. But I am a professor of supply chain management—logistics are supposed to be my specialty!

Since the engineering school's ceremony started earlier than the business college's, I thought I could pull it off and be at both events. I discussed this with John, and he agreed to let Grant move to the front of the line so I could give him his diploma and leave. If all went well, I would make it to the Walton College ceremony with fifteen minutes to spare.

Of course, all didn't go well.

The program for engineering began on schedule, but one of the speakers went over the allotted time and I began to sweat a little under my cap and gown. The clock ticked, and the speakers spoke. And spoke. And spoke. Finally, it was time to hand the students their diplomas, but the Walton College ceremony was due to start in just five minutes. I calmly handed Grant his papers, smiled for a photo, and then walked off stage, went out a side door, and raced to Bud Walton Arena.

I arrived as the last students were being seated, so I followed them onto the arena floor and stepped onto the platform just as if that was the way my entrance had been planned all along. Several of the event managers gave me the evil eye, but I couldn't blame them—we had more than a thousand students graduating and the arena was full of their friends and family.

Dwight D. Eisenhower famously said that plans are useless when preparing for battle, but planning is indispensable. It's like that as a dean. We can never stop planning, but we're always adjusting to the changing realities that are coming our way. And we're always moving from one high priority to the next, sometimes with little time to catch our breath in between.

That's what makes a balanced life, or harmony as some call it, so difficult. It's easy to get sucked into the tyranny of the urgent and never emerge, bouncing from this to that like a pinball and neglecting the things in life that keep us healthy, happy, and sane. I'm convinced, however, that all leaders need to prioritize some basics in their personal lives to get the most out of their professional lives. If we don't take care of ourselves, we won't be in a position to take care of others.

As you'll recall, *dean* came from the Latin *decanus*, meaning "chief of ten," so I want to close the book with my top ten priorities for staying balanced in the role of business school dean:

Sleep. We all need good sleep every night, but deans start their days early and end them late. Raising money, for instance, involves attending lots of dinners, some of which go late into the night. I remember one fund-raising dinner that lasted six hours. Plus, you have to get up early for breakfast and coffee meetings with benefactors. It's also not uncommon for serious internal issues to arise at inopportune times, requiring you to stay up late writing a response to an email or making calls to help put out fires.

Getting enough rest is a huge issue for leaders. A global study found that 42 percent of leaders average six hours or less of sleep, but that a lack of sleep results in poor judgment, lack of self-control, and impaired creativity, and that the negative impacts cascades across teams and cultures (Barnes 2018).

To help me consistently get the rest I need, I use an app called Sleep Cycle. You turn on the app, put your phone on your nightstand, and it monitors your sleep based on your breathing. It tells you when you went to bed, when you fell asleep, when you woke up in the night, when and how long you snored, the stages of your sleep cycle, and when you woke up in the morning.

I've used this app for a couple of years, and I average six-and-a-half hours of sleep—one hour shy of my goal. Sleep Cycle, however, has helped me move toward that goal by making me aware of trends. For example, if I eat or drink too late, I won't sleep as much. Red wine late in the evening hurts my sleep more than anything. And I don't sleep as well when I go to bed late.

Eat. When you eat a good number of your meals at banquets, luncheons, award dinners, conferences, and speaking engagements, it's easy to indulge in the wrong types of food or even over indulge in the right types of food. But lots of research shows that how we eat affects not only our health, but our performance (Friedman 2014; Glabska et al. 2020).

For health reasons, I switched to a mostly vegan diet. I say mostly because I eat a few ounces of fish once per week. Other than that, I don't eat meat or dairy. More restaurants offer vegan options, but it's still a challenge at many places. I have discovered that, especially at nicer restaurants, if you ask the server to tell the cook you are vegan, the cook will make something appropriate for you.

I also periodically do a five-day "fasting mimicking" diet as designed by Valter Longo, a professor at the University of Southern California. A fasting mimicking diet consists of natural healthy products and ingredients that effectively trick your body to enter fasting mode. Research has shown that this program can address aging, cancer, cardiovascular disease, and provide other benefits.[19]

Exercise. There's no shortage of evidence that indicates regular exercise makes us more productive and effective in many different ways. For instance, it improves our concentration, memory, mental stamina, and creativity, while reducing stress and our learning curve (Mandolesi et al. 2018; Friedman 2014).

I try to walk ten thousand steps per day and exercise a few times per week—weightlifting, biking, and stretching—but I rarely achieve all of this every week. I go to a local gym for weightlifting once or twice per week, and I really enjoy biking on the miles of paved bike trails in Northwest Arkansas.

---

19. Valter Longo's website, www.valterlongo.com/, has more information on his research and diet programs.

More serious bikers ride on the roads, but I'm too risk averse, so I tend to use biking for a combination of exercise and commuting. In July 2020, I began commuting to and from work on my bike almost every day, which is about a fifteen-mile round trip. And about once every two weeks I'll have a day of meetings in Bentonville, Arkansas, so I'll ride my bike about twenty-five miles north, meet with people for eight or nine hours, and ride back home.

The problem for deans, as well as many other leaders, is that the job comes with a travel schedule that tends to wreak havoc on an exercise routine. It seems that just when I get into a routine, I go into a season of travel and fall off my routine. But most hotels have a gym, and I can always do Pilates in my room, so there's really no excuse for not doing some sort of exercise even when I'm away from home.

Meditate. When leaders wake up knowing that their schedule includes a long list of challenges that are "urgent" to someone, it's hard to slow down the mind and calm the old amygdala in our brains so we can think creatively and fully consider the perspectives of everyone involved. Instead, our minds tend to race from one thought to another, as each competes for our attention.

It's tempting to start each day by diving into email as we wait for the clock to strike a time when it's appropriate to start making phone calls. But I have found from experience, and research backs this up, that beginning with some form of meditation/prayer sets me up for a more effective, less stress-filled day.

Exercise or even just relaxing around the house might take our minds off problems in a good way, but calm, intentional mindfulness actually improves our leadership. It builds our resilience, boosts our emotional intelligence, enhances our creativity, helps us focus, and improves our relationships (Seppala 2015).

Matthias Birk, an adjunct professor at New York University and Columbia Business School, says meditation allows us to "step out of our own survival centric thinking and connect with others empathetically. This is important, because research shows that when we get scared, we display greater egocentrism and it is harder for us to take other peoples' perspective" (Birk 2020).

I try to make it a habit to pray, read the Bible, and reflect quietly for a few minutes each morning. I actually have it on my calendar to remind me.

Unfortunately, many times I let the worries and opportunities of the day derail me.

Relate. Before you become a dean, you typically will have many friends who have no connection to your university or even to academia. After you become dean, however, you need to develop relationships with benefactors, your advisory board, alumni, administrators across campus, and others whose work connects them to your work. It is easy to let those other relationships wither.

There's great value, of course, in developing friendships at work; in fact, research shows there are a long list of benefits—people with strong social connections at work have been found to have better cognitive function, resilience, engagement, are less stressed, have better work-life balance, share ideas more freely, and are more likely to find purpose, meaning and a positive outlook about their work (Beard 2020).

While it's not always easy, I've also found specific benefits to maintaining friendships with people outside of work. They provide a diversity of opinions on issues, for instance, which broadens my perspective. Deans may find they have less time for purely social gatherings, but there are many ways to keep personal friendships active—attending community events, volunteering, meeting around common interests (like exercising), walking (and visiting) in your neighborhood, or spending time with friends at your faith community.

Stand. One of the best investments in office furniture I've ever made was my adjustable desk that allows me to stand while I am working. It isn't healthy to sit all day, and research has shown that standing can improve workers' productivity more than 40 percent (Garrett, G. et al. 2016).

I alternate between standing and sitting a few times per day. When I'm on a video call, I find I'm more engaged and alert when I'm standing. I seem to type faster when I'm standing, as well. I have plenty of meetings where I wind up sitting, so many days my desk never leaves stand-up mode because I only use it for a couple of hours.

Play. If you are saving your hobbies and vacations for retirement, you are doing a disservice to your health, your family, and your work. Of course, it is hard to find time to take vacations (especially as a dean), and it is also hard to find time for hobbies. But both are important for your success as a dean. Research shows clearly that we need breaks from work.

When I'm tempted to skip a vacation, I like to remind myself that Lin-Manuel Miranda came up with the Broadway musical *Hamilton* while he was on vacation. When we don't take vacations, our performance drops and so does our satisfaction with our work. Plus, we're less likely to get a raise (Zucker 2020).

When we're on vacation or just when we're at home with friends and family, playing games can not only help us relax from the stresses of our day but also help improve our strategic thinking. That's why gamification has become more popular as an approach to training and team-building, so it's not just something leaders should do when we're away from work (Reeves and Wittenburg 2015).

Say no. One of the first words we learn as a child is "no," and it seems we can spend the rest of our lives trying to actually use it appropriately. Many leaders, I've found, rise through the ranks because of their willingness to say yes to risks, to help others succeed, and to pursue new opportunities. But I've also experienced the adverse consequences that come from committing to too many good things rather than focusing on my big-rock priorities.

Brain Halligan, the CEO and co-founder of Hubspot, believes that saying no is a salient component of the art of strategy. I've already discussed how I use our mandate as a filter for decision making, and Halligan takes a similar approach with his one-page MSPOT document.

"With it," he says, "we articulate our Mission, the constituencies we Serve, the Plays we're going to run this year, the plays we are going to Omit, and how we will Track our progress" (Halligan 2018).

By saying no to things that don't align with our mission and priorities, we're in a better position to say yes to what matters most and what actually helps us and our teams achieve meaningful success. But we have to say no in the right ways. As author and social scientist Joseph Grenny points out, we need to share our logic, acknowledge the trade-offs involved, speak with confidence but without being harsh or insensitive, and honor the other people involved (Grenny 2019).

Learn. There's never a bad time to learn something new, especially about leadership. In fact, in my experience, truly effective leaders are always students of leadership. You can become a student of leadership by reading books and articles on leadership, reading biographies and autobiographies of leaders, listening to podcasts, observing leaders you work with, being mentored by other leaders, and mentoring up-and-coming leaders.

Everything on my schedule, as well as every impromptu situation, presents a learning opportunity. I learn from sitting in meetings, from having conversations with my wife and kids, from recording podcasts with other leaders, from walking in my neighborhood—from every experience—just as long as I do one key thing: Open my mind to learning from it.

Take what you learn and experiment with it. Keep the ideas, concepts, and techniques that work for you. But you have to continually learn, because situations change and the techniques that will work for you will change, as well.

Forgive. We have all been wronged, and we have all wronged others. Some people who have wronged us in the past can now help us make a better future for the college and should be forgiven. Engaging someone who has wronged you or recognizing their achievement are clear signals of forgiveness that go beyond words.

As Harvard Business School professor Resabeth Moss Kanter points out, revenge is neither justice nor strategy, and holding a grudge hurts the grudge holder more than anyone.

"Anger and blame are unproductive emotions that tie up energy in destroying rather than creating," Kanter said. "People who want to save a marriage, for example, must let go of the desire to hurt a partner the way they think the partner has hurt them and instead make a gesture of reconciliation" (Kanter 2013).

There you have it: Sleep, eat, exercise, meditate, relate, stand, play, say no, learn, and forgive. The basics of balance for any leader, but certainly for the dean of a business college.

I know, it sounds a bit like Robert Fulghum's list in *All I Really Need to Know I Learned in Kindergarten,* which, come to think of it, is certainly worth adding to any list of how to get the most out of life.

It was Fulghum, by the way, who said, "When you go out into the world, it is best to hold hands and stick together" (Fulghum 1990). Like all of his advice, that's good for deans, too, because while the basics are often pretty simple, they aren't always easy and we always need some help along the way.

I hope what I've shared in this book will make your journey easier. You'll encounter curves you can't anticipate, and you may take a detour or two along the way. But the rewards are priceless. Enjoy the journey.

I n my tenure as dean, I've witnessed the enormous generosity of our alumni, who have given both financially and with their time and wisdom.

Among other things, they have helped us launch the Little Rock executive education office, the Brewer Family Entrepreneurship Hub on the square in Fayetteville, the McMillon Innovation Studio on campus, the Supply Chain Policy Initiative, the William Dillard Department of Accounting, and the Blockchain Center of Excellence. Many of them also participate on one of my advisory boards—the Dean's Executive Advisory Board, the Dean's Alumni Advisory Council, and the Dean's Roundtable of Entrepreneurs and Market-Makers.

All these initiatives and boards serve as catalysts for transforming lives through our breadth of research, scholarship, creative activities, and an environment centered on learning. And, of course, they have been influential in my growth as a leader of the Walton College.

I am also thankful for our faculty, staff, and students for living our EPIC values (excellence, professionalism, innovation, and collegiality). These individuals inspire me daily to give my best and to find ways to improve because I know when I serve them well as dean, there is nothing they can't accomplish.

My wife, Susanne, and I married in 1986; she has made this entire journey possible and enjoyable. Together, we engage in entertaining all of my constituent groups, and she always encourages me.

Commitments of Department Chairs of the Walton College

Excellence

- Support the research and teaching missions of the college
- Build an environment that focuses on students and facilitates learning
- Secure resources for the department and college
- Identify and remove barriers to excellence
- Make decisions that best leverage both judgment and data

Professionalism

- Act and make decisions guided by the values of the college
- Ensure responsible stewardship of financial and other resources
- Allocate resources in a manner that supports the vision/mission of the university, the college and the department
- Advance department objectives simultaneously with the best interests of the college

Innovation

- Emphasize innovations that align with our strategic initiatives
- Challenge the college (our processes, people, systems) to adapt to the current environment as well as prepare strategically for the future.
- End initiatives that fail
- Encourage collaboration across departments and colleges

Collegiality

- Build a working environment that promotes honesty, integrity, credibility and trust
- Listen and display respect for each person in the college
- Speak encouraging words that build up others and discourage damaging characterizations of others
- Demonstrate ethical actions in all encounters
- Resolve problems at the lowest appropriate level in the organization
- Be willing to offer and receive constructive criticism

Commitments of the Dean and Associate Deans of the Walton College

Excellence

- Support the research mission of the college
- Build an environment that focuses on students and facilitates learning
- Develop philanthropic resources
- Secure resources for the college

Professionalism

- Act and make decisions guided by the values of the college
- Ensure responsible stewardship of financial and other resources
- Allocate resources in a manner that supports the vision/mission of the university and college
- Exhibit loyalty to the Walton College and its people, and to the university

Innovation

- Emphasize innovation that facilitates our strategic direction
- Challenge the college (our processes, people, systems)
- Span boundaries to identify opportunities and challenges
- End initiatives that fail

Collegiality

- Delegate without abdication
- Listen and display respect for each person in the college

- Speak encouraging words that build up others; discourage damaging characterizations of others
- Demonstrate ethical actions in all encounters
- Be willing to offer and receive constructive criticism

Leadership Framework

Copy and use this blank framework to evaluate any project or initiative, before, during, or after you launch.

		WHAT LEADERS DO		
		Setting Direction	Gaining Alignment	Providing Motivation
HOW LEADERS LEAD	Sensemaking			
	Relating			
	Visioning			
	Inventing			

Table A.1. Integrating the "What" and "How" of Leadership

Leadership Framework for Marketing

Our efforts at the Walton College to build a best-in-class public business school marketing program illustrate what it looks like to integrate the "what" and "how" of leadership. Table A.2 shows how that effort fits in my framework.

		WHAT LEADERS DO		
		Setting Direction	**Gaining Alignment**	**Providing Motivation**
HOW LEADERS LEAD	Sensemaking	Online programs are growing, MBA programs are generally in decline, some companies are not even requiring degrees, and credentialing firms are emerging. These trends are increasing the strategic importance of the brand of the business school.	Disruptions in higher education are a threat to all of us, but so is the trend of declining support of higher education by various states around the country. We need a marketing capability that can generate alternative sources of revenue for the college.	A strong marketing strategy and execution can benefit each faculty member, because a key part of the program will need to be the promotion of the personal brands of our most authoritative and influential faculty.
HOW LEADERS LEAD	Relating	We talked about developing an excellent marketing program with many faculty members in one-on-one meetings. These were conversations, not monologues. We also had extensive discussions with alumni and benefactors.	We needed buy-in from some of our most influential and well-known faculty. To that end, I met with several of them one-on-one and eventually formed a committee of faculty members who would become a part of our micro-influencer strategy of marketing.	I personally started to operate as a micro-influencer through social media and explained how it could be used by each of them. I also explained how it could benefit them by promoting their research, consulting, and teaching.

Table A.2. Building the Best Public Business School Marketing Program

		WHAT LEADERS DO		
		Setting Direction	**Gaining Alignment**	**Providing Motivation**
HOW LEADERS LEAD	Visioning	We secured some early wins, such as our experiment with #ThisIsHowWeIntern on LinkedIn. Although this was simple, it created a mental image of what is possible.	One of our most effective and profitable programs experienced a decrease in enrollment. We hired a marketing firm to conduct a secret shopper analysis on this program, as well as peer and aspirant programs. Then we showed people in the college the difference between what we were doing and the best practices of the other programs. The important realization is there are lots of great ideas about this process and most business schools are not using many of the best practices.	In talking through the isolated best practices of other programs, one thing became very clear—none of the best practices had very high barriers to entry. Not only we could emulate them, we could exceed them and have the best response system to inquiries about our program in the entire industry. This is motivating. Marketing at its core is about exchange and response to inquiries is a moderator of the effectiveness of exchange.
	Inventing	As far as we know, our micro-influencer strategy has not been done by any other business school, so we are plowing new ground by inventing this marketing strategy. Faculty and staff are involved, and all of them are inventing elements of the strategy.	As faculty, students, and staff members got involved with this program, more wanted to join, as well. We needed to ramp up more slowly as a result of the costs and our lack of business processes for onboarding new people.	The innovative personal branding created by this marketing strategy creates motivation for faculty, staff, and students. In addition, faculty, staff, and administrators of various programs see the effectiveness of the new strategy and see it as a way for their program to succeed.

Table A.2. (*Continued*)

Leadership Framework for Diversity and Inclusion

Developing Diversity and Inclusion is an ongoing commitment at the Walton College. Here are some ways I filter that commitment through my leadership framework.

		WHAT LEADERS DO		
		Setting Direction	**Gaining Alignment**	**Providing Motivation**
HOW LEADERS LEAD	**Sensemaking**	DEI is in our mission and one of our strategic initiatives. The leadership and the ODI continually explain the importance of DEI in the Executive Committee meetings and in other communications.	We need to continually and clearly articulate the importance of DEI to our college and the state. If we don't improve our DEI, then we will become less relevant and will not be fulfilling our vision and mission.	We have the Walton College Diversity Award. Faculty need to see how when they personally contribute to the college's DEI efforts, it helps specific faculty and students. Very specific examples can be motivating.
	Relating	The Walton College needs to develop a program for mentoring of new faculty and staff. We have opportunities and resources available which address the unique challenges faced by faculty who are women—Women of Walton.	We need to be purposeful in our networking with diverse groups in each of the business disciplines. We need to have diverse pools from which to draw guest speakers and academic talks.	Honorariums should be provided to professors from other universities who come to the Walton College to present academic research. We should expand BLA, Fleisher Scholars and ACAP.

Table A.3. Developing Diversity and Inclusion

		WHAT LEADERS DO		
		Setting Direction	Gaining Alignment	Providing Motivation
HOW LEADERS LEAD	Visioning	We are now coming up with a strategy to apply our powerful marketing processes to DEI, not only for the college but for the university.	Diversity plans for departments include recruitment strategies. We also participate in the Ph.D. project.	We need to collect data on faculty satisfaction with availability and quality of support services and professional development resources.
	Inventing	The director of ODI was given a seat on the Walton College Executive Committee. College promotion and tenure committee is required to complete implicit bias training.	We need to continue to develop effective relationships with partners to recruit prospective applicants from diverse backgrounds. Our community college collaboration is an effort in this direction.	We are encouraging the cultivation of a diverse candidate pool over time, not just during a specific recruitment initiative. This requires networking at academic conferences, for example. It could also include coauthoring research with a diverse set of coauthors.

Table A.3. (*Continued*)

REFERENCES

Chapter 1

Waller, M. (Host). 2019. *Be Epic, Episode 16: Dan Worrell* [podcast]. Fayetteville, Arkansas, University of Arkansas. https://walton.uark.edu/be-epic-podcast/dan-worrell.php.

Chapter 2

Armour, R. 1980. "A Little Etymology (Word Origins) for Discerning Readers." *The Christian Science Monitor* (December 8). Accessed November 2, 2018. https://www.csmonitor.com/1980/1208/120803.html.

Gee, K. 2018. "For U.S. Business Schools, Leaders Are Hard to Find." *The Wall Street Journal,* June 20.

June, A. W. 2018. "To Change a Campus, Talk to the Dean." *The Chronicle of Higher Education, October:* 5.

Sholderer, Olga. 2018. Email interview, November 9.

Chapter 3

Cable, D. and F. Vermeulen. 2018. "Making Work Meaningful: A Leader's Guide." McKinsey Quarterly, October 2018.

Northouse, Peter G. "Leadership: Theory and Practice." Sage Publications, 2018.

Chapter 4

Ancona, D., T. Malone, W. Orlikowski, and P. Senge. 2007. "In Praise of the Incomplete Leader," *Harvard Business Review*, February, 109–117.

Brooks, D. 2019. "Students Learn from People They Love: Putting Relationship Quality at the Center of Education." *The New York Times,* January 17. Accessed January 23, 2019. www.nytimes.com/2019/01/17/opinion/learning-emotion-education.html.

Kotter, J. 1990. "What Leaders Really Do," *Harvard Business Review*, 68, no. 3. (n 1990), 103–111. Reprint version (2001) accessed December 20, 2018. https://hbr.org/2001/12/what-leaders-really-do.

———. (1999) *John P. Kotter on What Leaders Really Do.* Harvard Business School Press.

Love, H. 2016. *The Start-Up J Curve: The Six Steps to Entrepreneurial Success.* Greenleaf Book Group Press.

Zaleznik, A. 1977. "Managers and Leaders: Are They Different?" Harvard
Business Review, 55, 67–78. Reprint version (2004) accessed December 20,
2018. https://hbr.org/2004/01/managers-and-leaders-are-they-different.

Chapter 5

Anand, V. 2019. "The Strengths of the Walton MBA Programs—The Full Time
MBA," LinkedIn.com, 12 February. https://www.linkedin.com/pulse
/strength-walton-mba-programs-full-time-vikas-anand/.
Byrne, J. 2019. "Why Business Schools Are Shutting Down Their MBA
Programs." Forbes.com, May 26.

Chapter 7

Maccoby, M. and T. Scudder. 2018. *The Leaders We Need,* 2nd ed., Harvard
Business Review Press.
Mautz, S. 2019. "Google Tried to Prove Managers Don't Matter. Instead, I
Discovered 10 Traits of the Very Best Ones," Inc.com, 5 June. Accessed 21 June
2019. https://www.inc.com/scott-mautz/google-tried-to-prove-managers
-dont-matter-instead-they-discovered-10-traits-of-very-best-ones.html.
Ryan, J. 2009. "Every CEO Must Be a Chief Listening Officer," Forbes.
com, December 30. Accessed June 21, 2019. https://www.forbes
.com/2009/12/30/chief-listening-officer-leadership-managing-ccl
.html#a86fcc379f58.
Leadership WWeb: The podcast. Chancellor Joseph E. Steinmetz, June 2019.
Soundcloud.com. Accessed August 14, 2019. https://soundcloud.com
/user-561194034/joseph-steinmetz.

Chapter 9

AMA.org. 2021. "Definitions of Marketing." Accessed January 18, 2021.
www.ama.org/the-definition-of-marketing/.
Jobs, S. 1997. "Best Marketing Strategy Ever! Steve Jobs Think Different / Crazy
Ones Speech (with Real Subtitles)." YouTube. Accessed October 20, 2019.
https://youtu.be/keCwRdbwNQY.

Chapter 10

Ziglar, Z. 1982. *See You at The Top,* 147. Accessed November 16, 2018. https://
archive.org/details/SeeYouAtTheTopByZigZiglar/page/n1.

Chapter 11

June, A. W. 2018. "To Change a Campus, Talk to the Dean," *The Chronicle of
Higher Education, October:* 5.

Neem, J. 2014. "How to Evaluate Academic Research," May 15, *Inside Higher Ed.* Accessed November 13, 2019. https://www.insidehighered.com/views/2014/05/15/dont-evaluate-scholarly-research-public-impact-alone-essay.

Chapter 12

Espinosa, L., J. Turk, M. Taylor, and H. Chessman. 2019. "Race and Ethnicity in Higher Education: A Status Report," February 2019. Accessed September 9, 2019. https://www.equityinhighered.org/.

Lorenzo, R., N. Voigt, M. Tsusaka, and M. Krentz. 2018. "How Diverse Leadership Teams Boost Innovation," January 23, 2018. Accessed September 20, 2019. www.bcg.com/en-us/publications/2018/how-diverse-leadership-teams-boost-innovation.aspx.

Phillips, K. 2017. "How Diversity Makes Us Smarter." *Greater Good Magazine,* September 18. https://greatergood.berkeley.edu/article/item/how_diversity_makes_us_smarter.

Speer, D. 2021. "Scholarship Honors Long-Time Leader of Walton College Office of Diversity and Inclusion," January 18, 2021. Accessed January 18, 2021. https://waltontoday.uark.edu/2021/01/18/scholarship-honors-long-time-leader-of-walton-college-office-of-diversity-and-inclusion/?fbclid=IwAR1SPy_CxyiBs-p5-R7o84U1k2RgFxKzCqtrdRbBZChnD—pNKcy3jeX8Xk.

Chapter 14

Waller, M. (Host). 2019. *Be Epic, Episode 10: Bill Dillard II* [podcast]. Fayetteville, Arkansas, University of Arkansas. https://walton.uark.edu/be-epic-podcast/bill-dillard-ii.php.

Chapter 15

MacArthur, J. 2013. *The MacArthur Study Bible,* in a note on 1 Corinthians 13:4–7.

Reward Gateway. 2018. "New Research Reveals Breakdown Between Employees and Employer in Recognition, Trust and Communication of Mission and Values," February 5. Accessed November 29, 2018. https://www.rewardgateway.com/press-releases/new-research-reveals-breakdown-between-employees-and-employer-in-recognition-trust-and-communication-of-mission-and-values.

Sanborn, M. 2018. "6 Ways You Can Be More Thoughtful," blog. Accessed December 28. marksanborn.com.

Chapter 16

Barnes, C. 2018. "Sleep Well, Lead Better." *Harvard Business Review,* September–October. Accessed January 22, 2021. https://hbr.org/2018/09 /sleep-well-lead-better.

Beard, A. 2020. "True Friends at Work," *Harvard Business Review,* July–August, Accessed January 23, 2021. https://hbr.org/2020/07/true-friends-at-work.

Birk, M. 2020. "Why Leaders Need Meditation Now More Than Ever," *Harvard Business Review,* March 22. Accessed January 25, 2021. https://hbr .org/2020/03/why-leaders-need-meditation-now-more-than-ever.

Friedman, R. 2014. "What You Eat Affects Your Productivity." *Harvard Business Review,* October 17. Accessed January 23, 2021. https://hbr.org/2014/10 /what-you-eat-affects-your-productivity.

Friedman, R. 2014. Regular Exercise Is Part of Your Job, *Harvard Business Review,* October 3. Accessed January 25, 2021. https://hbr.org/2014/10 /regular-exercise-is-part-of-your-job.

Fulghum, R. 1990. *All I Really Need to Know I Learned in Kindergarten.* New York: Villard Books, 6–7.

Garrett, G., et al. 2016. "Call Center Productivity Over 6 Months Following a Standing Desk Intervention." *IIE Transactions on Occupational Ergonomics and Human Factors,* vol. 2, no. 2–3. Accessed January 23, 2021. https://www .tandfonline.com/doi/abs/10.1080/21577323.2016.1183534.

Glabaska, D. et al. 2020. "Fruit and Vegetable Intake and Mental Health in Adults: A Systematic Review," *National Library of Medicine.* Accessed January 23, 2021. https://pubmed.ncbi.nlm.nih.gov/31906271/.

Grenny, J. 2019. "How to Say 'No' at Work Without Making Enemies." *Harvard Business Review,* August 5. Accessed January 25, 2021. https://hbr .org/2019/08/how-to-say-no-at-work-without-making-enemies.

Halligan, B. 2018. "The Art of Strategy Is About Knowing When to Say No." *Harvard Business Review,* January 26. Accessed January 25, 2021. https://hbr .org/2018/01/the-art-of-strategy-is-about-knowing-when-to-say-no.

Kanter, R. 2013. "Great Leaders Know When to Forgive," *Harvard Business Review,* February 26. Accessed January 25, 2021. https://hbr.org/2013/02 /great-leaders-know-when-to.

Mandolesi, L., et al. 2018. "Effects of Physical Exercise on Cognitive Functioning and Wellbeing: Biological and Psychological Benefits." *Frontiers in Psychology,* April 27. Accessed January 25, 2021. https://www.frontiersin.org /articles/10.3389/fpsyg.2018.00509/full.

Reeves, M. and G. Wittenburg. 2015. "Games Can Make You a Better Strategist," *Harvard Business Review,* September 7. Accessed January 25, 2021. https:// hbr.org/2015/09/games-can-make-you-a-better-strategist.

Seppala, E. 2015. "How Meditation Benefits CEOs," *Harvard Business Review,* December 14. Accessed January 25, 2021. https://hbr.org/2015/12/how-meditation-benefits-ceos.

Zucker, R. 2020. "Thinking of Skipping Vacation? Don't!" *Harvard Business Review,* August 11. Accessed January 25, 2021. https://hbr.org/2020/08/thinking-of-skipping-vacation-don't.

Note: Page numbers followed by *n* and number represent footnote and note number respectively.

Matthew A. Waller is the dean of the Sam M. Walton College of Business at the University of Arkansas, where he also serves as the Sam M. Walton Leadership Chair and a professor of Supply Chain Management.

Matt joined the UA as a visiting assistant professor in 1994 and has held several positions over more than twenty years with the college of business. He was the director of the executive MBA-China program for two years, and the chair of the Department of Supply Chain Management when it was established in 2011. He also was the recipient of the Council of Supply Chain Management Professionals' Distinguished Service Award in 2020.

In addition to his work in academia, Matt was cofounder and a partner with Bentonville Associates Ventures and cofounder and chief strategy officer for Mercari Technologies. A native of Kansas City, Mo., he graduated summa cum laude with a bachelor's degree in economics from the University of Missouri. Then he earned a master's degree in management science and a PhD in business logistics, both from Pennsylvania State University.

Matt is an SEC Academic Leadership Fellow, and has served on a number of local, university, state, and national boards. He currently is a board member for the nonprofit Winthrop Rockefeller Institute. He is coauthor of *The Definitive Guide to Inventory Management, Purple on the Inside: How J.B. Hunt Transport Set Itself Apart in a Field Full of Brown Cows,* and *Integrating Blockchain into Supply Chain Management: A Toolkit for Practical Implementation.* He is the former coeditor of the *Journal of Business Logistics,* the leading academic journal in the discipline.

Matt lives in Fayetteville, Arkansas, with his wife Susanne. They have four adult children.

Stephen Caldwell is a writer, editor, editorial consultant, and entrepreneur whose work appears on a range of platforms across a variety of markets. In a career that spans more than thirty years, Stephen has been a writer and editor for newspapers, magazines, and websites, collaborated on more than two dozen books, and developed leadership and functional training for Fortune 500 companies.

In his work with the Sam M. Walton College of Business at the University of Arkansas, Stephen is a frequent contributor to the Walton Insights blog platform and regularly works with professors to help transform academic papers into shorter articles that are more easily digestible for industry practitioners.

Stephen is the founder and chief word architect for WordBuilders Communications, an editorial consulting firm that helps leaders shape and effectively share their messages to broad audiences. His writing career began as a preteen, when he penned articles about Little League baseball games for the weekly newspaper owned by his family in Marianna, Arkansas. After college and a successful career as a sportswriter and columnist for the *Arkansas Democrat-Gazette,* he helped launch the award-winning magazine, *The Life@Work Journal.* He also has worked as a city editor for the *Democrat-Gazette* and as a director for a training development agency.

Stephen lives in Fayetteville, Arkansas. He and his wife, Audrey, have a blended family that includes seven children and sixteen grandchildren (at last count).

About the Walton College

The Sam M. Walton College of Business traces its roots to 1926 and has nationally competitive undergraduate and graduate programs. It consistently ranks among the top thirty best public colleges and the top fifty public or private colleges in America by *US News and World Report,* and its supply chain management undergraduate program is ranked No. 1 in North America by Gartner.

Under Matt Waller's leadership, the Walton College has raised more than $180 million since 2015; launched the McMillon Innovation Studio, the Brewer Family Entrepreneurship Hub, the Blockchain Center of Excellence, the Business Integrity Leadership Initiative, and the Customer Centric Leadership Initiative; expanded its executive education program to central Arkansas; become the host for the Supply Chain Hall of Fame; developed a new Department of Strategy, Entrepreneurship and Venture Innovation; and established four new master's degree programs.